The New Collar Workforce brings home the concept of how STEM education training — paired with the creativity and multi-disciplinary skill sets engendered through digital fabrication in the Fab Lab community — will lead to the perfectly positioned next-generation workforce. That workforce will face technologies we can't yet imagine, but it will be able to embrace those technologies and lead us into the future.

— *Sherry Lassiter, Director, Fab Foundation*

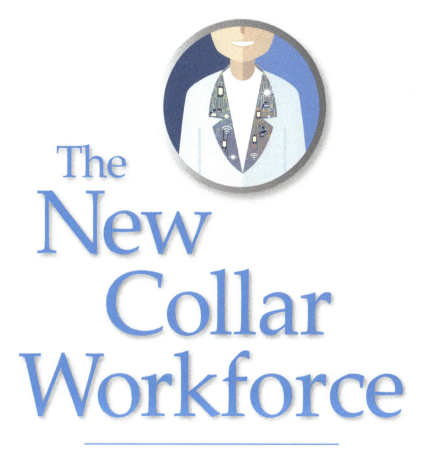

The
New
Collar
Workforce

An Insider's Guide to Making Impactful Change
in Manufacturing and Training

Sarah Boisvert

Photonics Media Press
Laurin Publishing Co., Inc.
P.O. Box 4949
Pittsfield, MA 01202-4949
U.S.A.

To see all titles in the Photonics Media Press library visit www.Photonics.com.

The New Collar Workforce
Cover illustration courtesy of Fab Lab Hub

ISBN: 978-0-9988539-9-4

Dedication
To Paul Christensen, Ph.D., who taught me
everything I know about laser physics

Acknowledgments

The research that serves as the basis for *The New Collar Workforce* was partially funded by a donation from the Verizon Foundation, without which this project would not have been possible. Of course, I am most grateful to the companies who took the time to talk with me about their workforce needs, sharing their views of manufacturing's future with candor.

I have learned so much from Sherry Lassiter, president of the Fab Foundation; Neil Gershenfeld, director of the MIT Center for Bits and Atoms; and the many creative people in the international Fab Lab Network whose work is an inspiration to us all.

In my current consulting work, Mike Adelstein and Potomac Photonics provide me with a link to real-world factory production. I appreciate Mike's discussions of all topics related to running a manufacturing company, which keep me current on the state of the art. Mike has taken our company and built it into the dream we always had for its future.

It has been a pleasure to work with Karen Newman and the Photonics Media Press staff, who I know are pushing the boundaries in technical publishing with this book, but who saw the importance of the topic for advanced manufacturing in the digital age.

With thanks to everyone!

Contents

INTRODUCTION

A Paradigm Shift in Manufacturing

I joined Potomac Photonics Inc., then in Lanham, Md., and now in Baltimore, to co-found the commercial manufacturing division of a pioneering laser R&D company. One day in 1986, Potomac Photonics's founder, Dr. Paul Christensen, predicted, "Someday people will email us design files and we'll laser micromachine their designs, then FedEx them finished parts." I thought he was crazy. After all, we used CompuServ for email back then and I could not imagine transferring a big computer-aided design (CAD) file via this crude service. But Dr. Christensen is a visionary, and he saw the future of digital fabrication, a cornerstone of today's advanced manufacturing. As he predicted, the digital age created a paradigm shift in manufacturing.

Thirty years later, previously unheard-of futuristic products can be made using cutting-edge processes such as 3D printing. But above all, manufacturing has morphed into a fully integrated digital operation that is iterative, dynamic, people-centric and agile, creating opportunities for a workforce that is engaged in furthering both its own immediate reality and the future of work. In the meantime, traditional blue

1

collar jobs have languished, and education's emphasis has shifted to a goal of everyone earning a college degree, making it easier to find an engineer than a machinist. Today, we find ourselves living and working in an era of fast-paced global upheaval in manufacturing that is often called the Fourth Industrial Revolution — a term coined by World Economic Forum founder Klaus Schwab. This new manufacturing uses advanced sensors, feedback loops, generative design, automation, robots, the Internet of Things (IoT) and a myriad of other exciting new tools that integrate the digital, biological and physical worlds.

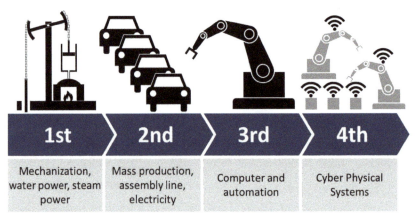

The Four Industrial Revolutions (by Christoph Roser at AllAboutLean.com).

CHAPTER ONE
Defining the Skills Gap

Manufacturing today can quickly create new products, deliver them more efficiently and with better customer satisfaction than in the past, and in the process, show higher productivity that yields greater profitability. However, as next-generation technologies have converged in modern-day digital manufacturing and new opportunities have emerged in a wide range of industries, the number of skilled workers needed to fill manufacturing jobs has dwindled. Blue collar jobs have evolved into digital new collar jobs, but the training for workers has not changed.

The manufacturing industry first started to take seriously the reality of a skills gap when President Barack Obama's Council of Advisors on Science and Technology released a report[1] in 2012 based on data from the U.S. Department of Labor[2]. Shockingly, projections estimated a shortfall of 2 million skilled manufacturing workers by the year 2020. The reality of that statistic, like all economic indicators, is complex and has fueled debate as to whether or not the skills gap actually exists. Additional studies from that same period, as well as more recent research, provide overwhelming evidence that the difficulty in finding an operator or technician is not an isolated case.

This much seems clear:
- Manufacturers continue to rank talent as the most critical driver of global manufacturing competitiveness, according to the 2016 Global Manufacturing Competitiveness Index[3] compiled by Deloitte Touche Tohmatsu Ltd. (Deloitte Global) and the Council on Competitiveness in the U.S. It is, after all, people who innovate, and not machines.

- Baby boomers in key manufacturing jobs, such as machinists, are reaching retirement age. According to The Manufacturing Institute and Deloitte, in 2015 approximately 22 percent of the existing workforce is over 55 years of age and eligible to retire in the next 10 years. This represents 2.7 million open jobs that employers need to fill[4].

- But insufficient numbers of young people are taking their jobs. The same study conducted by Deloitte for The Manufacturing Institute found that in 2015 employers in the manufacturing sector saw 60 percent of their open jobs unfilled since they could not find workers with the necessary skills for the positions. For those jobs that they were able to fill, the recruitment period for skilled production workers was 70 days[5].

- The 2016/2017 Manpower Group Talent Shortage Survey collected data from more than 42,300 employers in 43 countries and territories and reported that 40 percent of employers responding were having difficulty filling jobs — the highest proportion since 2007. Skilled trades such as welding or plumbing were the hardest jobs to fill for the fifth consecutive year. Production/machine operators, technicians, IT staff and engineers were all in the top 10[6].

But as we dig into the details behind these facts, we find that the world's top manufacturing countries are investing heavily in technology for advanced manufacturing, suggesting an increasing need for skilled workers. CEOs in the U.S., China, Germany, Japan and the United Kingdom ranked the future importance of advanced manufacturing technologies, shown in the graph on the opposite page.

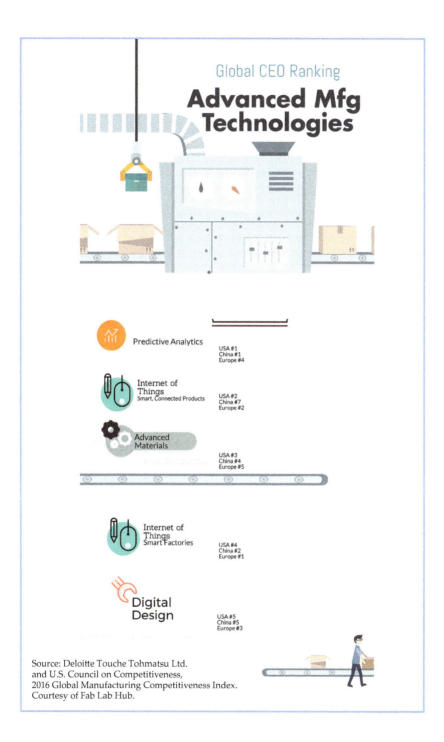

Global CEO Ranking

Advanced Mfg Technologies

Predictive Analytics
USA #1
China #1
Europe #4

Internet of Things
Smart, Connected Products
USA #2
China #7
Europe #2

Advanced Materials
USA #3
China #4
Europe #5

Internet of Things
Smart Factories
USA #4
China #2
Europe #1

Digital Design
USA #5
China #5
Europe #3

Source: Deloitte Touche Tohmatsu Ltd.
and U.S. Council on Competitiveness,
2016 Global Manufacturing Competitiveness Index.
Courtesy of Fab Lab Hub.

New Skills Needed for our Technical Age

Jobs in these advanced manufacturing technologies require higher-level STEM (science-technology-engineering-math) and STEAM (STEM + the arts) skills than traditional manufacturing jobs. We are living in an age of smart manufacturing that is being called Industry 4.0 because of its reliance on high-tech systems, sensors, feedback loops and information-capturing systems that collect large amounts of data (big data) in running modern factories. While some machining work is still manual, equipment is increasingly digitally driven by CAD files. Plus, popular quality programs such as Lean, which grew out of the Toyota Production System for efficient manufacturing and the ISO Quality Management System from the International Organization for Standardization, require ever-more-sophisticated measurement tools.

That said, because of automation, an engineer or a Ph.D. holder may not be needed to make a specific part. That, in turn, means that operators and technicians must function at a higher technical level to run the digital tool. For example, to drill a hole, laser machining requires the use of optics to focus the light coming out of the laser to the desired "spot size" of concentrated energy. Usually, the size of the hole varies from job to job, so each time a spot-size change is needed, the configuration of the optics has to be modified and manually rebuilt. Today, a machine tool's autofocus feature implements this task, much like autofocus in a digital camera. However, operators need to know how to correctly set up and adjust the parts, and in some cases, program the parameters, perform post-processing cleaning and accurately measure the finished part to meet customer specs.

Recently, I had the bright idea to put my tabletop 3D printer on a cart and wheel it to a classroom for a presentation. The MakerBot is an extrusion-type printer, so the print head from which material is extruded needs to stay at a constant distance from the build plate where material is deposited. Many tabletop 3D printers now have auto-leveling to ensure that the distance is uniform, a process that is easily accomplished through a software command sequence on the control screen. We auto-level the build plate before each print, but when I started the 3D printer for a live demonstration, auto-leveling failed. The floor had not been as smooth as I thought, and the Z-axis was so far out of alignment that I had to go through a complete manual process to align the build plate with the print head. Fortunately, the MakerBot Replicator+ had excellent instructions in its digital display, and the alignment was done quickly, but it required a higher level of technical skill than just selecting the auto-leveling button.

In 2012, Thomas Friedman, who writes about foreign affairs, globalization and technology for *The New York Times*, examined the worker needs of a small manufacturing business based in Minnesota. As the company moved into the aerospace and military markets, the standard welding it had previously provided no longer satisfied customer standards. While welders might have been able to make a beautiful weld, to manufacture these high-tech products, they also needed to understand the science behind welding, metallurgy, modern cleaning and post-processing techniques, and how different metals and gases, pressures and temperatures had to be combined to meet specifications. A welder needed to be able to read and understand design drawings, which were now digital. Friedman drove home how far manufacturing job skills had come: "Who knew? Welding is now a STEM job — that is, a job that requires knowledge of science, technology, engineering and math [7]."

And that was way back in 2012. Each year, the requirements for manufacturing operators and technicians become more demanding as technology becomes more sophisticated, further broadening the skills gap. Yes, manufacturers are looking for machinists. But these are not your grandparents' or even your parents' generation of workers. To be competitive in a global market, manufacturers today need staff with digital fabrication skills deeply rooted in 21st-century STEM subjects.

Middle Skills Bridge the Gap

"Middle skill" is a relatively new term for work that demands higher levels of technical skill than were previously required but does not require a four-year engineering or science degree. Often, two-year associate degrees, digital badges, on-the-job training, internships, co-ops or apprenticeships are sufficient to qualify for these jobs.

A 2012 *Harvard Business Review* article estimated that "as many as 25 million, or 47 percent, of all new job openings from 2010 to 2020 would fall into the middle-skill range[8]." Further, wages were higher, with accompanying opportunity for advancement into lifelong careers. In 2016, the Associated Black Charities and the Greater Baltimore Committee conducted a study on pathways to middle-skill STEM careers for inner-city residents. The study reported that in 2011, workers in middle-skill STEM occupations earned 61 percent more than workers in non-STEM occupations with similar levels of education. The average wage for middle-skill STEM workers was $58,504 a year, which was above the 2015 annual living wage of $52,998 in Baltimore. And of all STEM jobs available in the Baltimore area, 43.3 percent required middle-skill levels of training[9]. This tracks national averages compiled by the U.S. Department of Commerce. Manufacturing employers who hire middle-skills workers also provide medical benefits, and more important, many fund on-the-job training and pay for external training. A few even offer scholarships for college degrees.

CHAPTER TWO
Manufacturing's Current Image

Besides the need for more technically skilled workers, manufacturing also has an image problem. A poll conducted in 2010 by the Foundation of the Fabricators & Manufacturers Association (FMA) yielded a 52 percent response from teens that they had little or no interest in a manufacturing career. Another 21 percent were ambivalent. The main reason from a solid 61 percent of the respondents was that they seek a "professional career," with a meager 17 percent mentioning lower pay. After all, according to the teens, manufacturing is a dirty job conducted in a dangerous environment where workers are not required to think, personal growth is discouraged and there is little opportunity for career advancement[10]. That certainly doesn't sound like a "professional career."

A recent study did show that Americans see manufacturing as a high tech field — but in the future. Recent digital manufacturing advances are not recognized in the general population and sadly, only 43% of the respondents see manufacturing jobs as interesting and professionally rewarding. Perhaps factory layoffs making the news – due to the large number of people affected — led 72% to think manufacturing jobs are not stable. Only 21% of those queried actually knew that manufacturing jobs are increasingly available and accessible[11].

Perhaps even worse, the Society of Manufacturing Engineers (SME) conducted a study clearly demonstrating that parents were not encouraging their children to pursue careers in manufacturing for exactly these same reasons. Parents want their offspring to have bright futures as doctors, lawyers, Wall Street executives and Fortune 500 CEOs. Less than 40 percent of the parents polled viewed manufacturing as a well-paying profession, and 20 percent saw manufacturing as offering outdated, dirty and unhealthy work, harking back to the first industrial revolution of the late 1700s [12].

Most of the parents interviewed who wanted their kids to be "professionals" didn't see a future in industrial careers. For the past few generations, working in manufacturing jobs has had a stigma. As described by Joan Williams in her book, "White Working Class," the professional class looks down on those who didn't go to college, deriding their blue-collar work but also their lifestyles, which include close-knit families, religious connections and conservative values. Yet these are the people who build their cars and process the oil that fuels them. Is it any wonder that in the 2016 election, President Donald Trump appealed to a group that felt financially left behind but also undervalued by the elites?

That same year, the Massachusetts Executive Office of Housing and Economic Development sponsored research on recruiting people into manufacturing. An interesting side finding by the Wentworth Institute of Technology Innovation Fellows in Boston, who conducted the study, was the intrinsic desire of millennials to work in fields that provide a high level of positive social impact. Manufacturing doesn't convey that image, even though manufacturing technology gives us the eco-friendly electric Tesla car, microfluidic devices for rapid cancer diagnostics, 3D printing of customized prosthetics, and robots that take over dangerous tasks in disaster zones[13].

I have to say that as a woman who works in manufacturing, using cool tools like lasers and 3D printers, I have a lot of credibility interacting with the younger high-school and college generation. They don't see me as they see their parents, but rather as someone in tune with what's happening today through our connection with the digital technologies that they themselves use or see in their online world. My 3D-printed earrings are always a hit and open many conversations about my hip life in digital manufacturing.

CHAPTER THREE
New Collar Jobs

Coined by IBM CEO Ginni Rometty, the term "new collar" jobs perfectly sums up the kinds of workers manufacturers need today and into the future. What matters most is relevant skills, sometimes obtained through vocational training, she wrote in 2016, imploring President-elect Donald Trump to look toward the factory of the future and not backward to old-school factory models. At some IBM facilities in the U.S., she explained, as many as a third of the employees needed less than a college degree to successfully meet job requirements[14].

New collar is certainly a more engaging term than middle-skill, and it captures the imagination of the students and parents who are looking toward career options. Manufacturing today taps into the natural skills of digital natives, the young people who have grown up with smartphones, social media, video games and GPS. These 21st-century abilities are imperative to run automation and software, design in CAD, program sensors, maintain robots, and collect and analyze data — all skills that are needed to work in Industry 4.0.

Further, we are looking to a generation that has grown up hearing the Silicon Valley success stories of company founders such as Steve Jobs of Apple and Bill Gates of Microsoft, neither of whom finished college. Open doors for these young people, and who knows what they might accomplish.

CHAPTER FOUR
The Courage to Change

We live in truly exciting times for manufacturing. The cool, futuristic technologies that are driving Industry 4.0 hold enormous promise for the future of manufacturing. But it is the new collar worker who embodies the creativity, curiosity, drive to have an impact in the world, and natural digital competence that will rejuvenate an industry that is out of touch with the times. Manufacturing has long been a conservative industry, but we must find the courage to innovate and to initiate change, embracing the ideals and aspirations of a new generation of factory workers who can help lead us into a prosperous future. In turn, new collar jobs hold the promise of higher wages that can support a family. They elevate the social status of workers in communities where manufacturing has had a long and powerful history. Survival of our very companies, as well as the middle class, depends on this. If we cannot find the courage to change the status quo, the health and well-being of our entire socio-economic system is at risk.

How do we accomplish this tall task? To seize the manufacturing opportunity that is upon us, first we must expose our youth, veterans, and especially women and minorities to the new collar job possibilities prevalent in Industry 4.0 today and demonstrate what they mean for tomorrow. Then, we must build and support new training programs that answer Industry 4.0's demands in a way that makes sense for both today's workers and employers. Investment from government and industry is essential to reshape the workforce training landscape. But if we are to be competitive in manufacturing, we cannot depend on old industries that are quickly being replaced with new models. The buzz phrase in today's management schools says, "Uberize your company or you'll get Kodaked!" The urgency cannot be downplayed. I heard Harvard Business School professor Michael Porter speak many years ago, and one phrase in his talk stuck with me: "Strategy is not doing more of the same thing." Manufacturing can be revived if we take Porter's advice and fashion completely new strategies to innovate immediately with new collar job training for Industry 4.0.

The following chapters offer a guide to making impactful change in manufacturing. I describe technologies found in the "smart factory" of today and tomorrow, explain the new collar job skills needed to use its new tools, and provide examples of highly innovative training programs that are emerging to break the mold of traditional manufacturing workforce development.

PART ONE

This is NOT Your Father's Factory Floor

People who do not work in industry think advanced manufacturing means new technology such as 3D printing. But to those of us who actually manufacture parts day in and day out, advanced or "smart" manufacturing in Industry 4.0 is a complex integration of equipment, processes, software, data collection and people in order to improve quality, increase productivity, drive down costs and create an engaged workforce.

A wide range of new technologies form the foundation of Industry 4.0, driving innovation and our ability to manufacture smarter, faster, more economically and with less waste. That requires a totally new skill set for the new collar jobs today and into the future.

CHAPTER FIVE
The Factory of the Future

The idea of future factories being operated 100 percent by robots generates fear in the mainstream media, but such a radical change is unfounded, at least for the immediate future. While robots are working more frequently alongside humans, someone still has to design, program, maintain and service automation tools — at least for now. Artificial intelligence allows robots to "learn," but in today's factory, human capability is still required. The digital aspects of Industry 4.0 create high demand for humans working as CAD designers, software coders, digital equipment operators and technicians, and data collection analysts.

In some industries, the factory of the future is already here. Just look inside a semiconductor fabrication plant or a MEMS (micro-electrical-mechanical system) chip foundry where manufacturing equipment operators have worked in clean rooms wearing high-tech "bunny suits" and shoe covers for decades. This environment is far

Digital Equipment Operator

Big Data Analyst

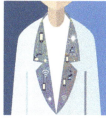

Robot Programmer

CAD Designer

Lean Implementer

3D Printer Repair Technician

Courtesy of Fab Lab Hub.

from dirty. An automotive industry production line looks nothing like one from the days of the Model T. Robot-operated laser cutters are ubiquitous on the production lines at GM and Ford, and Chevrolet's Corvette line is a prime consumer of laser welding equipment. These changes were just the first steps toward Industry 4.0.

We are now experiencing a radical increase in the velocity and scope of change, which is affecting entire systems. Groups such as Singularity University, a Silicon Valley think tank and innovation incubator, have found that every aspect of human endeavor is being transformed by exponential growth. Singularity's annual Exponential Manufacturing Summit brings together thought leaders who are harnessing the power of this extremely rapid change to create the manufacturing models of the future. From the start-up, Made In Space Inc., 3D printing replacement parts on the International Space Station, to Local Motors's crowdsourcing of a user-friendly mobility device for a variety of physical impairments, exponential thinking is in many cases a few (or many!) years out.

While some of these progressive companies are racing headlong into a new manufacturing future, many factories are not yet fully embracing change. As I visit manufacturers, my fear is that they are oblivious to the forces at work and will be blindsided in a few years by the innovators who will take away their customers and employees in a new manufacturing model. The current state of Industry 4.0 seems to be somewhere between these two extremes. Most manufacturing executives say they know that incorporating new technologies and processes is important to stay competitive and have added some basic digital tools to the factory floor. But the changes are limited in depth and scope, and rarely incorporate radically new technology, processes, workforce training or ways of thinking. Here are some successful models of complete Industry 4.0 implementation.

CHAPTER SIX
GE Brilliant Factory

General Electric is taking manufacturing beyond smart and advanced to brilliant. It was GE that first brought to my attention significant changes on the factory floor. At a wide variety of industry conferences and trade shows over the past few years, I have heard GE executives and researchers evangelizing about the power of new factory models through keynote speeches and technical presentations to their manufacturing colleagues.

With over 500 factories around the world and ranking 13th on the Fortune 100 list, GE has the strength to lead manufacturing to Industry 4.0 with its Brilliant Factory. The company manufactures in a wide range of industries including oil and gas, health care, lighting, aviation, energy, power and transportation, giving it a broad understanding of manufacturing processes. According to Philippe Cochet, GE's senior vice president and chief productivity officer, "Gone are the days of the dirty old factory; today it is about advanced technology and innovation"[15].

GE has seen solid results through implementation of the Brilliant Factory concept. At a GE Transportation facility in Grove City, Pa., unplanned downtime — equipment failures that shut down production — was reduced by 10 to 20 percent. When considering the cost of keeping a production line in operation, these are significant percentages. High investment in additive manufacturing (AM) has also yielded strong return on investment in the CFM International* LEAP fuel nozzle tip, with a decreased parts count, increased durability and reduced weight.

The software and hardware, processes and methodologies used in the Brilliant Factory have presented GE with another business sector

19

opportunity: GE Digital. Based on the Predix Industrial internet platform that links machines, software and people in the Brilliant Factory, GE Digital now offers products and services to companies in manufacturing and other industries that need full hardware, software and process integration to achieve Industry 4.0 success. Customers are reporting significant reductions in inventory, improved quality measures and faster time to market using the Brilliant Factory concepts and tools. GE also is now selling metal 3D printers that are optimized for production, no small feat in the technically challenging area of additive processing.

Four Pillars of the GE Brilliant Factory

It is my perception based on live presentations and my own interviews with GE executives that GE built the Brilliant Factory based on four areas in which they have extensive experience:

- Lean principles and processes
- Additive manufacturing and automation equipment
- Industrial internet
- Predictive analytics from big data

Lean Principles

Starting in the late 1980s, legendary CEO Jack Welch set out to make GE the quality leader in every product the company manufactured. He instituted a learning culture and borrowed heavily from the Toyota Production System, which is the basis of Lean principles and methods.

He decided in 1995 to implement Six Sigma — data-driven defect elimination — at GE, inspired by the remarkable results achieved by Motorola. Though he may not have been 100 percent convinced about the practical results of Six Sigma, Welch was impressed by the concept and strategies. It is interesting for today's Smart Factory that General Electric started with a heavy emphasis on training the workforce for data-based problem analysis, which is necessary when measuring and reducing defects.

Joe Rizzo, the founder of Lean is Green and the New England Lean Consortium, ran three small factories for GE using Lean principles, and he interacted with Jack Welch before the formal programs began. In a conversation I had with Joe, he shared with me a few principles about the GE Six Sigma program:

Value. Our job is essentially to create value for the customer. To give the customer the value for which they are willing to pay, we must obviously listen to their needs, but that is easier said than done. Value may mean fast delivery or zero defects. But it is the customer's value of the product or service we are creating, not our own. Often, I would find engineers over-designing a product for a customer. My analogy in discussion with our team was this: If the customer is looking for a Honda to get them reliably to work, we should not deliver a Lamborghini. And as a business owner, customers were not willing to pay for sports cars when all they wanted was transportation.

Value Stream. The total value of all activities in the product life cycle involves measuring added value versus non-value-added activities. This is a tough concept for most people, as many things don't add value but are necessary. State and federal laws, for example, may require safety activities, but they do not alter raw materials into a finished product. To eliminate waste, we need to optimize all actions that add value and carefully look at how we can minimize or eliminate non-value-added activities.

Flow. Continuous one-piece, straight-line flow of the product through the production process is essential to eliminate waste. Anything, for example, that has to go back for re-work disrupts flow and wastes time, materials and ultimately money. If it delays delivery, customer service time may be required and future sales may be lost.

Pull. Producing to the pull of the customer rather than building up inventory is a fundamental concept in Toyota's Just-in-Time inventory philosophy. Obviously, it is only a highly skilled factory with strong Lean principles that can pull off JIT, which requires good collaboration between departments, minimal waste, strong planning and excellent vendor relationships.

Perfection. Elimination of waste in the system is the ultimate Lean goal, and measurements such as Six Sigma approximate perfection. Lean companies aim for high standards in product quality. In doing so, Lean also generates a number of additional benefits, including solid industry reputation, the ability to attract talented staff, and pricing advantages over competitors.

People-oriented. Lean motivates total employee engagement to help with problem solving and generating ideas for continuous improvement. Staff that are engaged at work are noticeably more productive and become active contributors to the health of their careers.

Lean principles that were intrinsic to GE manufacturing are even more prominent in the Brilliant Factory. The risk of increased failures and waste grow as technologies become more sophisticated and integrated. Even better manufacturing processes are needed to keep factories up and running at peak performance.

Additive and Advanced Manufacturing Equipment

GE has one of the most aggressive and visible additive manufacturing/3D printing programs in the world, investing heavily in the machines, materials and processes needed to move the technology to industrial applications. There are currently over 400 3D printers in use across GE factories, with heavy utilization of metal additive manufacturing technologies. Beyond the cool factor seen in the press or the hype about everyday people making prosthetic limbs in their kitchens, there are serious reasons that 3D printing is an important tool in the Brilliant Factory.

Rapid prototyping was one of the earliest applications of additive manufacturing, mostly because early machines were too slow for production. However, getting functional prototypes that require no assembly right out of the machine is still highly useful in turning around fast proof-of-concept prototypes for new product development.

The aerospace industry's smaller volume production benefits substantially from the ability to print complex geometries that reduce weight. Airbus has stated that it is seeing an average 55 percent weight reduction in 3D-printed parts, which, of course, has a direct correlation to fuel consumption. GE has a large aircraft engine business and the 3D-printed nozzles in its LEAP engine are 25 percent lighter than those that are traditionally fabricated.

3D printing

The ability to print complete designs reduces parts counts and consequently, inventory carrying costs, a big consideration in Lean principles. The CFM International* LEAP fuel nozzle tip combines 20 parts into one, yielding five times more durability than traditional fabrication. Adding rather than subtracting material greatly reduces waste, one of the prime goals of Lean manufacturing. Think of the amount of waste material that subtractive milling or machining leaves on the factory floor. Astonishingly, aerospace companies have measured as much as 70 percent lower material costs due to complete material usage in a 3D printing process.

Automation

Automation in the GE Brilliant Factory is more than robots performing repetitive tasks. Industrial automation is part of an Industrial Internet Control System that integrates automated performance of machines, software and processes. For example, managing modern wind farms that may have thousands of turbines requires remote control systems that can respond to environmental factors on the fly.

Just as the World Wide Web links personal computers around the globe, the Industrial Internet (a term coined by GE) provides interconnectedness to individual production machines operating in the same plant or thousands of miles away. Results can be used for remote retrieval, allowing parameters to be better managed and resulting in greater productivity. Just as the consumer world demands instant gratification from connected devices, the industrial world now demands instant information to make quick decisions on the factory floor.

Big Data and Predictive Analytics

Not surprisingly, GE's Brilliant Factory doesn't just collect data for immediate reactions to factory conditions. The huge amount of data gained from sensors embedded in machines, software reporting and all integrated data collection systems in the Industrial Internet are harvested so that humans can learn from the process. By using statistical programs, data can be mined and then modeled to look at risks and opportunities from actual historical experience. Predictive analytics can save a production line from repeat errors, eliminating costly surprise downtime and increasing productivity, and, ultimately, profitability.

Big data in a factory is the start of true machine learning, which increases a tool's value as part of the production line. In the Deloitte study referenced earlier, CEOs in both the United States and China listed predictive analytics as the most important technology for securing global manufacturing competitiveness. Manufacturing is inherently a conservative industry, as change is often quite costly and worse yet, disruptive. Industrial managers strive for predictability; consequently, any tool that can predict with some accuracy what can be expected from machines, software, production lines and people is a huge help in achieving goals.

The Factory as a System

Every single element in the Brilliant Factory is tied together by what GE calls "the digital thread."

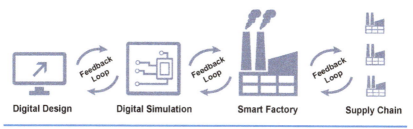

Digital Design   **Digital Simulation**   **Smart Factory**   **Supply Chain**

Factory as a system. Chart by Devon Unwin.

The digital thread weaves digital capabilities through all the technologies in the Brilliant Factory, as well as externally to the supply chain and ultimately to customers. It is a fully integrated digital manufacturing system that pulls together the entire Brilliant Factory concept.

A key element of the digital thread is expanded virtual capability, which the industry has dubbed "the digital twin." In the past, products and their parts were created virtually in CAD and modeled in software. Today, tapping into big data supplied by the Internet of Things, or IoT, in the interconnected factory, entire manufacturing processes can be created virtually, allowing managers to see how machines are performing and to review product specification matches such as color, hardness or size. Digital twins can be created for products in the field, as well as for goods in process in the factory, which is especially useful for large-scale products such as airplanes and container ships. By replicating what is happening on the factory floor, the digital twin is a fast and economical method for designing and testing improvements to the system before physical implementation.

CHAPTER SEVEN
Industry 4.0 Beyond GE

According to the B2B research firm MarketsandMarkets, the size of the worldwide market for "smart factory" tools, software and technologies in 2016 was valued at $121 billion and is expected to reach $205.42 billion by 2022, growing at a compound annual growth rate of 9.3 percent between 2017 and 2022. MarketsandMarkets predicts that the growth of this market is "propelled by the increase in adoption of industrial robots, and the evolution of Internet of Things (IoT)"[16]. As in any market of this size, there is a tremendous amount of investment as corporations see the fast pace of change and the opportunity it brings. The largest activity in the market is in the Asia Pacific region –– China, Japan, India –– followed by North America, then Europe. But the U.S. and Germany are investing heavily, and some predict they will overtake China shortly.

In Europe, Siemens relies on automation to lead its Industry 4.0 factory transformations. In its Amberg electronics plant in Germany, production quality is currently at 99.99885 percent; an intensive test process catches the few defects that occur. These statistics are impressive given that the factory manufactures 12 million Simatic products per year. Siemens's Digital Enterprise Platform has automated the entire manufacturing process with software that allows parts to communicate their individual manufacturing processes to the production machines with accurate specs and in correct order for building the finished product. Amazingly, approximately 50 million pieces of process information are generated each day from the production lines — a true example of big data. The data is then stored in the Simatic IT manufacturing execution system to further improve processes through predictive analytics.

The benefits are exponential. In a white paper, Siemens interviewed 60 industrial manufacturers, academics and management consultants in 11 countries to measure productivity gains in all manufacturing. Siemens estimated what it calls the "digitalization productivity bonus" to be between 6.3 percent and 9.8 percent of total annual revenue by 2025. This is a significant increase for valuing the switch to the digitally based Smart Factory[17].

GE has partnered with other U.S. technology giants including AT&T, Cisco Systems, Intel and IBM to create the Industrial Internet Consortium. This nonprofit organization is creating a framework for companies, university researchers and thought leaders to establish standards and best practices for industrial applications of the internet in Smart Factories. Started in 2012, the nonprofit Smart Manufacturing Leadership Coalition similarly works to foster the implementation of Industry 4.0 in small, medium and large companies by providing open-source platforms and marketplaces. Collaboration is indeed a hallmark of smart manufacturing, as many smaller companies feel they can't make the transition to Industry 4.0 in isolation.

Advanced Manufacturing Technologies That Require New Collar Workers

Entirely new categories of jobs that didn't exist even a few years ago are now the mainstay of the new collar workforce because of the advanced manufacturing technologies of Industry 4.0. These range from creating sophisticated designs in complex software to programming robots and repairing 3D printers to running big data modeling programs. These jobs are in clean, safe environments and are in high demand with commensurate compensation and benefits.

While our earlier description of the Siemens Amberg electronics plant makes it sound as if it is run 100 percent by machines and software, in fact, humans are an important part of the monitoring and decision making that occurs in the highly automated process. Digital machines may operate the test stations, but the hardware must be managed by a human electronics technician, who monitors the hardware, software and processes from his or her computer. This is one of the new collar jobs that didn't previously exist in manufacturing but that requires a tech-savvy, engaged worker with strong STEM skills. The next section describes several technologies in factories today that demand a new kind of workforce.

Next Generation Design

All digital manufacturing begins with a design that is created in computer-aided design (CAD) software. In its simplest form, the CAD files are then converted to machine code that drives the digital machines, telling them where to take away (cut, drill) or add (3D print) material. Industry leader Autodesk developed products in the 1980s that are still the backbone for many product designers. However, it is continually pushing the envelope, especially with collaborative software such as Fusion 360 that functions in the cloud, and other platforms that include modeling, product design, simulation and inspection. Often, one program is not enough to carry a product from prototype to production. Bundles of software tools integrate every aspect of the product life cycle, leading to seamless processes.

Current CAD software is intuitive and user-friendly for digital natives, especially if they've played computer games such as Minecraft. A part can only be as good as the CAD file from which a machinist or 3D printing technician is working. Digital fabrication requires that the operator or technician be able to read CAD files and make any corrections or modifications necessary to create the best part, since efficiency of the operation is tied back to parameters inherent in the design.

Just as initiatives such as An Hour of Code promote the idea that computer science and programming should be available to all students, I would argue that CAD skills are the foundation for any work today in manufacturing and should be included in all STEM education programs.

Computer-aided manufacturing, or CAM, takes CAD one step further, laying out digital instructions for machine operation, including the toolpath for the specific additive or subtractive machine. Efficient toolpaths add to quality as machining time is minimized, wear and tear on the tool is reduced, and extraneous movement is eliminated. Packages integrating CAD/CAM are common, creating seamless workflow, and new capabilities such as modeling, sculpting, simulation and visualization are continually added to base platforms.

One of the more compelling innovations in design software adds actual sensory communication between the digital world and the designer's body. Companies such as Geomagic (part of 3D Systems Corp.) include these so-called haptic tools with software to give designers a true feel for the product they are creating. This is especially useful for a surgeon, who can participate in the design for the best feel of a scalpel or other medical device through actual physical feedback of force, friction or stiffness from the software to the haptic design tool in his or her hand. Experience with haptic capabilities is especially useful for anyone building prototypes or at the early stages of product design.

Generative Design

"If you had all the computing power in the world, how would you design and build things differently?" That is the question Carl Bass, former CEO of 3D design software giant Autodesk and an innovative designer/maker in his own right, asked at The Digital Factory Conference hosted by 3D printing company Formlabs at the MIT Media Lab in June 2017. Bass argued that we now have infinite, cheap computing power and need to turn around the idea that computing power is a scarce commodity. This premise is the basis of generative design, where man and machines become co-creators.

In its infancy, generative design basically takes the input parameters a designer specifies, such as size, material and weight restrictions, to create an endless number of design possibilities. In the image below are just three possible designs, which you can see are quite different from each other, created by the Autodesk Dreamcatcher generative design research project from identical input parameters using internal algorithms. The manufacturer can then decide which design best meets its needs and discard the rest.

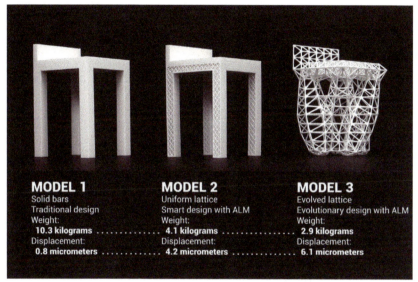

MODEL 1
Solid bars
Traditional design
Weight:
  10.3 kilograms
Displacement:
  0.8 micrometers

MODEL 2
Uniform lattice
Smart design with ALM
Weight:
  4.1 kilograms
Displacement:
  4.2 micrometers

MODEL 3
Evolved lattice
Evolutionary design with ALM
Weight:
  2.9 kilograms
Displacement:
  6.1 micrometers

Chair options using generative design software from Autodesk. Courtesy of Autodesk.

"The use of digital fabrication in advanced manufacturing rewrites the laws of the industrial revolution" said Bass, "and it is the application of the microprocessor [that] allows us to do all this. Now we can use machine learning to design as well as machine parts." Of course, generative design allows humans to design things that were difficult to do any other way and that have not yet been historically imagined, opening an as-yet-unexplored product development future. Bass imagines infinite uptime on the factory floor: "As sensors have become cheaper they can be built into machines to close the loop. We control the means of production, in order to have a more powerful factory of the future."

A bridge to full generative design comes in the form of a clever phone app that simplifies design changes. At Incite Focus, Detroit, founder Blair Evans has seen a transition in the making mindset in the past few years. Evans explained that today people are coming into the inner city fab lab (a digital fabrication laboratory) wanting to make things they need or want, but they don't necessarily want to be a maker. Makers tend to be most interested in the process of making, but many people just want to use the tools, not build, program and fix them. Evans said, "If we truly want to democratize access to the tools of digital fabrication, then we need to empower people in order to make stuff, not be a maker."

In his book "Crossing the Chasm," Geoff Moore described the leap necessary to sell high-tech products to mainstream markets. While early adopters of a new technology enjoy making the gadget work, mainstream markets want the device to work for them, helping them to complete tasks easily and quickly. Personally, I hated all the programming required to make my Blackberry functional, while my iPhone is mindless and serves my need to make phone calls, check email, listen to music or do anything else for which there's an app.

And an app, it was decided, was the best solution for this new generation of makers.

"Someone can go directly into CAD tools that are great today, but there is a lot of generality, so to narrow down choices for your needs takes a lot of expertise," said Evans. "A new user must be willing to go through a long learning curve, but that's not the majority of our people today." The app embodies the parametric design concepts and structural understanding — such as the strength of the object — and allows one to directly interact with the characteristics they want to produce. As a result, a maker can customize a design without having to do any raw coding. The app also integrates the ability to design with workflow and connects to the machine's G-code programming language.

Jonathan Ward, who had been a student at MIT's Center for Bits and Atoms where Fab Lab was born and who now works with Blair at Incite Focus, added, "We developed the apps in order to reduce the learning curve. The user can customize height or size easily. Right now we have two apps: one to make tables and the other is a house-framing app to build houses that automates cutting parts, even with standard hand tools."

Like many things coming out of the maker movement, the new apps are open source. Incite Focus is devising ways to add value such as providing design services or actually building table parts in order to fund future production.

3D Scanning

Similar to the way a camera captures a photo, 3D scanning captures a digital representation of a physical object. The technology has gotten more press attention in recent years because of its application in 3D printing applications. Need a spare part for a home appliance? Just 3D scan the old one, create a CAD file to feed into your home 3D printer and you never need the Maytag repairman again. While the premise is accurate in theory, there is a significant amount of skill that goes into 3D scanning for professional and manufacturing applications.

3D scanning apps for smartphones can scan simple objects, but for complex shapes, sophisticated technology and a significant amount of digital post-processing is essential. Take, for example, the human ear. The ear's complex shape and contours make scanning with simple tools very challenging. Direct Dimensions, Baltimore, a pioneer in 3D scanning, can accurately scan the ear and other body parts, and the company works with physicians to design natural-looking prosthetic facial features for patients who have had cancer, disease or trauma.

Michael Raphael, founder and CEO of Direct Dimensions, said applications for 3D scanning fall into four categories:

- Industrial 3D scanning that requires "hardcore CAD skill."
- Architectural 3D scanning of facilities for Building Infor-

mation Modeling (BIM) databases and creating traditional blueprint drawings.

- 3D scans of art in museums or historic pieces such as the Liberty Bell for study or archival preservation.
- Creation of animations for movies, commercials or video games.

On the industrial 3D scanning side, reverse engineering and inspection are the most commonly used applications. By scanning an existing part, a CAD file can be created and an exact duplicate of the part can be fabricated with either additive or subtractive manufacturing methods. Inspection applications include comparing the original CAD model to a finished part to check for deviations as part of a quality control process or to simulate and identify how parts will fit together in their real-world assembly. Of particular interest to Industry 4.0 is on-machine inspection that measures key features and makes changes in real time while the piece or tool is still in the production process.

Perhaps more than any other advanced manufacturing technology, 3D scanning is a unique blend of art and engineering requiring the eye of a photographer, the mechanical experience of an engineer and the digital skills of a computer programmer.

The Internet of Things

"What if a part, or an entire system like a car or a plane, could participate in its own design?" provocatively asked Mickey McManus, a pioneer in the field of collaborative innovation, human-centered design and education. In addition to being chairman of the board and a principle at MAYA Design, McManus holds nine patents in the area of connected products, vehicles and services that qualify him to know a bit about the Internet of Things.

At the 2017 Society of Manufacturing Engineers rapid prototyping conference (RAPID), McManus explained that the Internet of Things

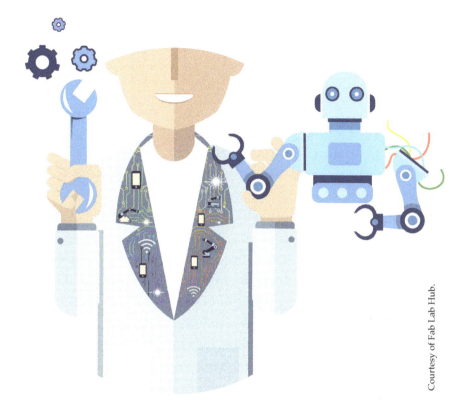

Courtesy of Fab Lab Hub.

would soon number trillions of connected devices communicating not only with each other but also with us. For humans to thrive in the emerging information system, the challenge is to connect the IoT with digital manufacturing and machine learning. And that is the operative concept: Humans pull the IoT together, conduct the big data analyses, monitor machine changes in response to their environment and make the final decisions regarding the entire system. It follows that workers must be conversant in both hardware and software, as the two now are inextricably linked.

The IoT requires not only sensor programmers and monitors, data collection specialists and analysts, and production line operators and technicians, but also an entirely new layer of security that must be addressed. Machines connected via the internet are open to hacking and security breaches, requiring workers to build, program, monitor and maintain cyber security systems for the IoT. With hacking in the modern world a given, opportunities in security forensics also are showing up on job boards.

Predictive Analytics

Historical analysis of data has been used for many years in the insurance industry to determine risk factors, which is helpful when calculating insurance premiums. In more recent times, political election campaigns and marketing programs mine data to predict consumer behavior. Consequently, statistical analysis tools already exist, and more are being developed specific to manufacturing. Anyone with a bent toward statistics now can find a new collar job in manufacturing. Further, big data is so complex because of the amount of information being collected that new software tools are conducting more complex functions, giving managers more user-friendly reports for decision making.

Predictive analytics affects four main areas in manufacturing applications: improving quality, accurately forecasting sales demand, optimizing equipment utilization and scheduling preventive maintenance. What these have in common is the direct ability to reduce expenses for a manufacturing company, making jobs in predictive analytics important to its financial health. In a 2015 joint study conducted by *Industry Week* and SAS, an analytics company based in Cary, N.C., 64 percent of executives said that their companies rely more on management experience than data analysis to make key decisions[20] but that they are getting increased pressure from upper management — and I would guess shareholders — to improve data analytics and make it an integral part of the manufacturing process, given the potential returns. All the top enterprise software companies, including IBM, SAS, HP and Oracle, offer predictive analytics software packages that can be easily integrated with other enterprise functions.

Machine Learning and Artificial Intelligence

While machine learning and artificial intelligence (AI) conjure images from science fiction, in fact, both technologies are all around us today. Have you ever wondered how the U.S. Postal Service can read all those addresses written in dreadful penmanship? Pattern recognition is a machine learning capability that helps sort the mail. Speech recognition systems and translation, as well as credit card fraud detection, all use machine learning. Patterns can be analyzed and models created many times faster by machine learning computer algorithms than by humans. IBM's Watson, the supercomputer that has beaten many a chess master at a human game, is an excellent example of AI. Incidentally, on a visit to IBM, the company gave me a lovely cookbook that Watson "wrote," although I wonder if other chefs would give up the sensory pleasure of tasting their creations. That brings up, of course, the artificial nose being researched in the Center for Bits and Atoms at MIT to detect smells for human safety applications. Autonomous vehicles are a hot AI topic right now, with ethicists debating how to program a myriad of decisions into cars and trucks.

Machine learning and AI have also found serious application in smart manufacturing. Since machine learning uses a number of statistical analysis methodologies and techniques, it is often applied in predictive analysis work. Neural networks, for example, can model very complex sets of data and find relationships to predict future outcomes, such as when a machine will fail. Optical parts sorting, failure detection, and many aspects of automation use machine learning, AI or both. One could make the case that machine learning and AI are what make smart manufacturing, well, smart.

Automation and Robotics

Automation via robots certainly is taking jobs from humans, but more often than not it is also creating new opportunities. As I like to point out, at least in the present time, humans need to design, program, troubleshoot, maintain and service robotic tools on the factory floor. In the past, safety costs to protect humans had sometimes been higher than the price of the robot itself. With the advent of sensors and the IoT, robots are better able to safely co-work with humans.

Manufacturing robots are ubiquitous in the fabrication, assembly, warehousing, packaging, painting and dispensing areas of the automotive, medical device, electronics, biotech and consumer products manufacturing industries. The new collar skills described earlier play into the successful implementation of robotics on the factory floor in these applications.

Courtesy of Fab Lab Hub.

In recent years, robots have found their way into new applications such as surgery, geriatric companionship and military operations. Because of the underlying occupational skills first required by these end-users, new jobs also exist in training and developing training materials for nurses, therapists and military personnel in the safe and efficient use of robots.

But there are many jobs for which robots cannot yet substitute for humans. Leading a team of people takes more than organizing time or allocating tasks. The subtle understanding of what motivates workers, or empathy, is not yet attainable by a machine. Creativity and innovation are other characteristics that robots lack. Apple's cool design innovations turned its users into fans and evangelists, although the superior user interface did help convert some customers. Spotting a trend in another industry and adapting it for a new market segment requires human observation and innovative thinking, as do the complex sales negotiations of high-value products such as laser machine tools. Often, reluctance to make a big equipment purchase has nothing to do with the measureable features of the machine such as feature size, cut quality or processing speed. I recall listening carefully to a buyer at lunch and discovering that his greatest fear was making the wrong choice of vendor and looking incompetent to his superiors. Robots don't eat lunch when on sales calls, which is ostensibly a cost savings, but in my experience a lot of valuable information is shared during social events or golf games.

Harnessing automation to free humans to do what they do best is perhaps the most powerful goal in industry today. Automation and robots in the early 21st century are more like enabling rather than replacement technologies.

3D Printing

Additive manufacturing has the potential to transform how things are manufactured but it is not yet the "Star Trek" replicator. That is good news for job seekers who have an inclination to work in the field, as significant operator knowledge and experience currently are essential to producing good parts using the relatively new technology.

Invented in 1983 by Chuck Hall, the founder of 3D Systems Corp., 3D printing still cannot replace all manufacturing processes. Because of constraints in speed and material selection, it is used only in select circumstances. Rapid prototyping was one of the first practical 3D printing applications, and 3D is still an excellent choice for producing prototypes, especially functional models that don't need assembly and work right out of the printer. Mass customization, that is, the 3D printing of many single personalized parts, is ideal for the technology's parameters. Since every human is different, medical applications such as Invisalign dental braces take advantage of 3D printing's special capability of economically producing one copy of a design. Because material is added and not subtracted, complex geometries that are impossible to machine can affect part characteristics such as shape and weight. For low-volume applications where weight is a substantial factor, such as in manufacturing aircraft, 3D printing is having a big impact.

Production 3D printing is just starting to take off. In 2016, HP introduced a production 3D printer that it says is cost competitive with injection molding at 50,000 parts. However, a main issue with 3D printing is that different additive technologies are needed to process

each category of materials. A plastic desktop 3D printer cannot make metal parts and vice versa, so separate machines are needed for each material category requirement.

These characteristics mean an entirely different approach to design has to be taken, espe-

Morris Technologies 3D printed metal aerospace part. Photo: S. Boisvert, courtesy of Greg Morris.

cially when replacing a traditionally manufactured part. A CAD file for a subtractive method doesn't take into account elements such as complex geometries. Design for 3D printing is unique and each type of 3D printing process is different, so the printer category being used must also be factored into the design. Designers who are conversant in 3D printing technology are needed for these applications.

Much of the challenge in dealing with design files was inherent in the open-source file format developed by Chuck Hall and his team when additive manufacturing was invented in 1983. Back then, color 3D printing in a wide variety of materials wasn't possible, so the STL file format used in 3D printing does not take colors, texture or materials into account when formulating the triangulations on which 3D printing files are built. As the technology has expanded to include many more parameters, the file format is woefully inadequate. A Cornell University group led by engineering professor Hod Lipson (he is now at Columbia University) had been trying to convene industry technical leaders to agree on a next-generation solution, but they didn't make much progress. We still must work around the limitations of STL 3D printing.

3D printing has created new collar jobs for operators, technicians, on-site service techs, customer service remote phone and online support techs, and 3D printing-specific CAD designers. In my experience, customers purchasing the new technology are not aware of the labor-intensive side to the machines, and when they ask me to suggest a more reliable or easier-to-use printer, I usually suggest they find an intern or dedicated employee with the specialized skills necessary to get and keep 3D printers up and running reliably.

New Manufacturing's Materials

Advances in materials have come from two major fronts. First, scientists are creating entirely new types of matter based on research in nanotechnology, biology and physics. For example, improvements in carbon fiber fabrication processes led to composites that are created by bonding the 5- to 10-micron carbon fiber strands with a plastic to form a carbon fiber reinforced polymer (CFRP). Carbon fiber composites exhibit superior qualities, such as high tensile strength, low thermal expansion, high stiffness and low weight. For industries such as aerospace, where every ounce of weight translates to fuel consumption, the high cost of carbon fiber composites is easily justified.

While carbon fiber is often at the top of the new materials list due to its strong application in a wide variety of products, other new materials are coming to the forefront. Conductive inks made of silver nanoparticles were used by Potomac Photonics in a National Science Foundation contract to build miniaturized sensors and other microelectronic devices. Optomec has built a strong business manufacturing conformal printed antennas for mobile devices, as well as embedded sensors for connecting products in the IoT. Biomimicry imitates aspects of nature for new materials. University researchers in many agricultural states are searching for ways to use crops such as potatoes, corn or wheat gluten to make bioplastics that would replace petroleum-based materials. Harvard University's Hansjörg Wyss Institute for Biologically Inspired Engineering looks to the natural world for materials. One of its most advanced projects is Shrilk, a compostable, clear and flexible material derived from silk proteins that is as strong as aluminum.

Materials science is both adding new job types and increasing performance requirements for current jobs. Machining with lasers, for example, requires that the machinist understand light's interaction with each type of material in order to choose the best wavelength for a job. Often, when someone tells me laser processing a material doesn't work, the issue is the specific wavelength choice, not the laser technology itself. Nanoparticles that are added to materials often alter characteristics that impact material performance, and new composites behave differently than the materials from which they are formed.

The second driver of Industry 4.0 materials is additive manufacturing. To secure approvals from regulatory agencies, 3D-printed parts for aerospace, aviation, automotive and medical device products must meet stringent government guidelines confirming to the designer or end users that a product made from 3D-printed material will perform the same as one manufactured by a traditional method. At the 2016 Rapid Conference, Christine Furstoss, vice president and technical director of manufacturing and materials technologies for GE Global Research, told me that "additive manufacturing has not yet harnessed the power of metallurgy. We need to look more closely at the chemistry and morphology to determine things like what it is going to take to not have so much post-processing for metal 3D-printed parts. Since I'm a powder metallurgist by training, I wish there was more emphasis on materials, but apart from my personal interest, the lack of information we have today puts serious limitations on where we can apply additive manufacturing."

Furstoss pointed out that certified parts need the best, most consistent properties, although some industries such as automotive can take more variability than, say, aerospace, where part performance is more critical to safety. She also said that while in-situ inspection being developed at places like Oak Ridge National Lab is a good start, there are limitations to it, and in many cases problems are detected at a late stage in the build, ruining a multiple-hour run. Material understanding will help us put in place stronger process parameters that will turn out parts with predictable outcomes. "The fuel nozzle in the LEAP engine is a static part produced in Auburn, Ala., but because of variability in the process, every part needs to be CT scanned. There is still enough performance benefit to choose 3D printing for the part, but since people's lives are at risk when they fly, we must put safety first," she said.

New job types are being created for work on 3D printing materials. Currently, research labs in universities, industry and government institutes are conducting materials characterization tests on 3D-printed parts in order to ensure that designers and engineers can predict performance. These labs utilize technicians to perform testing under the supervision of researchers. Manufacturers who use 3D printing also need operators and technicians who have experience with a wide range of new materials not seen before on the factory floor. One example that comes to mind is the biocompatible filament Enviro™ being produced by 3D Printlife. Additives in their ABS material are attractive to the microbes in modern landfills, speeding up the decomposition process. While I have had good results with 3D Printlife filament, operating parameters may not be identical to other material for a specific machine and the operator needs to understand how to modify settings.

Simulation

Simulation is an important technology utilized in Industry 4.0, at least until material and process understanding of AM is adequate for manufacturing's demands. A major frustration in 3D printing is the sur-

Biocompatible 3D printing filament. Courtesy of 3D Printlife.

prise one finds when the finished part comes out of the machine. Even designers who can identify specific problems at the CAD level will be surprised with outcomes when parameters such as layer thickness or material are changed in the machine. Predictability and repeatability are important in manufacturing. Even when prototyping, iterative design cannot work unless the characteristics we want to keep unchanged can be reproduced while adding modifications.

Tim Gornet, manager of operations at the University of Louisville's Rapid Prototyping Center, said that simulation software has to catch up to production 3D printers. Good products exist for injection molding and casting but not for 3D printing, especially when printing metal parts. As anyone who has ever 3D-printed knows all too well, the first- time failure rate is very high. To gain acceptance in industry the technology needs to improve its ability to consistently build parts that pass quality inspection. While trial and error is fun in the maker movement or to teach STEM skills in school, surprises are frowned on in production. Gornet explained, "Sure, we scan finished parts, but that's after the fact. Simulation can help us understand what we need to control in the AM process — how many variables are there, and of those, which are important to creating the best finished part. For metals this is essential, since they are used in more mission-critical applications. Plastics are rarely used in structural things where safety is an issue." All machines are different, with unique operating parameters, and Gornet pointed out that often what goes on in AM is counterintuitive, especially for those who have worked in subtractive processes.

Most metal additive manufacturing processes start with metal powders, and whenever any metal powder is melted you'll get shrinkage with variation in the wall thickness. The laser's heat also adds thermal stresses to the part, and Gornet reported seeing as much as 2 mm of deformation due to internal stresses in the material. The thermal stresses need to be calculated in advance as the parts will deform and warp if not held down via supports. This of course begs the question, "Where do you put the supports?" Part orientation can also have significant impact on print results. Gornet used the example of an ink pen that deforms when printed in the plane horizontal to the build plate. If one can simulate printing a particular design, these questions are answered. Re-design accomplished before the part is fabricated saves time, material and, obviously, cost.

Realizing the market opportunity, several start-ups and large software companies are introducing products in the simulation space. 3DSim, based in Salt Lake City, combines complex mathematical tools to create accurate simulations. French software giant Dassault Systemes has integrated simulation software with other products such as its popular Solidworks CAD design program to create a comprehensive 3D experience platform, taking products from concept to production. Using Dassault's Abaqus simulation software, BMW has been working toward moving automotive rapid prototyping to zero-prototyping. Crash testing is particularly time-intensive and costly, given the size of cars and trucks and the increasing government safety regulations that new vehicles must adhere to. The ability to move the BMW 6 Series Gran Coupé through virtual passive safety tests eliminates crash tests and speeds time to market. Simulation software is more advanced than basic CAD programming and design. Operators and technicians with skills in this new area will find job opportunities in advanced manufacturing, especially when metal 3D printers are in use.

Augmented, Virtual and Assisted Reality

Enhancing how we see the real world with computer-generated input assists the new manufacturing workforce in a wide variety of tasks. Enhanced or "augmented" reality, or AR, can be used in visualization, to align parts in a set-up procedure, or to locate a part for assembly in a warehouse. AR has been used for decades in sportscasting; just think of the lines drawn on the screen in American football to show where the ball is measured in relationship to a first down. AR can also add an interactive dimension to the real world. The option of opening a link to video instructions or an electrical circuit schematic in order to service a machine, for example, is a form of AR. Advanced use in manufacturing includes monitoring process improvements in real time. Language translation of signage and instructions is also possible using AR. In visiting a large U.S. beer bottling plant many years ago to troubleshoot a laser failure problem, the vice president of operations conceded that maintenance procedures were often not followed because workers had language barriers. Both for domestic sales, and export, equipment manufacturers can meet language translation needs with AR.

In its earliest form, AR that was developed by the U.S. Air Force in 1992 was complex and required considerable assistive devices, such as an exoskeleton worn by the user. AR has become ubiquitous in 21st-century smartphone and tablet devices, making adoption on the factory floor easy for digital natives. AR applications that reside on a device can "read" the instructions from the hardware link and quickly display requested data for the factory worker.

If AR enhances the real world, virtual reality, or VR, replaces it with a simulated, computer-generated world. Wearing an assistive device such as a headset, the VR user can interact with the virtual world via the sensorial feedback he or she experiences. VR, which grew out of interactive video games, is especially useful in training simulations. The software designer Autodesk is integrating VR with design software for engineering and architecture/construction. Taking VR further, companies can test concepts, designs and prototypes before they are even built. Ford Motor Co. has been pioneering VR in its design process using the Oculus Rift, a popular VR platform. A team from Autodesk research and the University of Manitoba has created Project Ivy that merges VR with the IoT. The resulting immersive programming tool allows the designer to interact with sensors and other smart devices in a room-size VR space, seeing exactly how data can affect tools or building infrastructure. For example, sensors can be programmed to reduce power to a museum display based on foot traffic in the immediate area.

Perhaps a more viable option for manufacturing is assisted reality, to which Google Glass has evolved. As often happens when new technology hits a mainstream market, the product was not 100 percent designed for reliable use by everyday consumers, and the social environment is not yet ready to adopt radical change. Google Glass being early to market was too far ahead of its time and faced exactly these mainstream market introduction issues. Strong rejection by users who had poor quality experiences and privacy concerns by the general public resulted in Google putting Glass Explorer on hold in 2015.

But in the last few years of the market test, Google realized that big manufacturing companies like Boeing were buying the product even without any industrial marketing sales effort. Further, developers were creating custom software to allow Google Glass to work specifically for the manufacturing space. In visiting the Boeing factory, Google immediately saw the potential of assisted reality on the factory floor. It revised the product with features that most benefited the manufacturing market[18]. In July 2017, Google launched Glass Enterprise Edition (Glass EE).

Manufacturing and surgical applications make practical sense since the user needs both hands free to work while accessing the real-time information that assisted reality provides. The Glass EE platform is certainly lighter and more comfortable than a full headset, as well as less expensive for the employer. But quality improvements that usually translate to added dollars on the bottom line were an unexpected benefit of assisted reality provided by Glass EE. A recent *Harvard Business Review* article reported a 34 percent performance improvement the first time a GE worker used smart glasses[19]. In the example, instructions to wire a wind turbine's controls were superimposed on the job by the AR smart glasses platform. Using data collected from GE and other large manufacturing firms, the article's authors (Magid Abraham, executive chairman of industrial software for the AR smart glasses provider Upskill and GE's chief economist Marco Annunziata) estimated an average 32 percent productivity improvement industrywide.

Assisted reality is a growing trend in manufacturing. Forrester Research predicted that by 2025, over 14 million workers in the United States will be wearing smart glasses like the Google Glass EE. It's another example of humans and automated technology co-working, yielding stronger results that neither could achieve alone[20].

Cybersecurity

With all of the interconnectedness on the internet or in the cloud, cybersecurity is a real concern today. And it isn't only financial information that can be compromised. Medical records are a growing area of big data that will only increase as sensors record health information directly from the body. In manufacturing, industrial espionage has moved to the digital age. Sensitive data about production methods, customers and marketing plans could be hacked by international competitors.

In a recent study, the recruiter Indeed.com found a lack of skilled applicants for many open jobs in the cybersecurity field. In the study,

Cisco cited 1 million unfilled cybersecurity jobs worldwide, and Symantec estimated that by 2019 the number will grow to 1.5 million[23]. Cybersecurity requires a skillset that combines broad technical knowledge with specific security expertise and a strong understanding of business risk. Globally, "network security specialist" is the leading category unfilled jobs. While there is much discussion of safety in the cloud, it appears that companies are most worried about their own internal networks.

Blockchain

While most of us think of blockchain technology in the financial world, this globally distributed ledger where things of value can be stored and moved securely and privately has enormous implications for manufacturing. The mass collaboration of blockchain builds trust and allows for verification of transactions with no cost. The Internet of Things will need blockchains to manage what is predicted to be trillions of daily transactions.

Supply chains are natural candidates for blockchain systems. Certifying a part or material, ensuring compliance with government regulations and verifying point of origin or manufacture are but a few of the issues that current supply-chain management struggles to ensure is accurate and provided economically. Blockchain in the future may be able to demonstrate the environmental impact of producing a certain product as well as provide anti-counterfeiting solutions.

In the supply chain, vendors and customers will have a transparent relationship with fewer middlemen, speeding transactions to increase efficiency.

Blockchain offers 3D printing users an answer to several problems. For groups of users like the U.S. Navy or humanitarian missions, sharing validated processes from initial design to post-processing is essential to ensure manufacturability in every scenario. The intellectual property ownership of 3D-printed parts always comes up in discussions of the technology's widespread adoption in mainstream markets. With blockchain, IP holders could tag their information so that it would always be a part of the ledger's data, protecting the IP. Although 3D printing has been a step toward distributed manufacturing, for most craftspeople there is still an intermediary. Etsy or Thingiverse, for example, are popular internet marketplaces for crafts, but transactions still go through PayPal, a bank or a credit-card processing company. Blockchain eliminates barriers to direct contact with customers, enabling truly open markets.

4D Printing

A few years ago, I heard MIT's Skylar Tibbits ask a question that pushed the boundaries of digital fabrication: "Can we make things that make themselves?" It boggles the mind. But on the practical side, rather than throwing things away, what if we instructed programmable materials to self-assemble into something else that we need? The Self-Assembly Lab that Tibbits co-directs has demonstrated the feasibility of this at least on a small scale. 4D printing may be in the future but it will undoubtedly change how we manufacture.

PART TWO

New Technologies Demand Different Skills

In 1997, Potomac Photonics needed to add sales personnel. One resume stood out, and when I brought the prospect, Mike Adelstein, in for an interview, he displayed a passion for technology, customer caring and a willingness to learn that could not be beat. He aced the written exam that I gave every salesperson. It required him to read an article aimed at a general audience that Potomac Photonics had produced for a trade journal, and condense it to an abstract of a few paragraphs. He demonstrated writing skills but also content understanding and analytical thinking ability. Potomac Photonics is a laser micromachining company, so some people were surprised that I would hire someone with a B.S. in biochemistry and molecular biology rather than engineering or physics. But I was interested in someone who could learn our evolving product line and solve problems for our customers. When he rolled up his sleeves to help us produce a job in one weekend, I knew I had made the right choice. Mike ended up leading a management buyout from Potomac Photonics's new owners in 2012, and he is now president and CEO, taking the company to a new level of advanced manufacturing contract services.

While technical competency is certainly essential for manufacturing jobs, in my mind, problem solving, curiosity and willingness to learn top the list of specific requirements needed for Industry 4.0. These skills are especially important for new collar workers, particularly operators, technicians, quality control staff and trainers, as well as marketing, sales and support staff. The new technologies of Industry 4.0, described in the previous chapters, require new collar workers to possess an entirely new skill set than what was required from blue collar or even white collar workers in the past.

In a 2012 TalentLens report, mechanical reasoning, logic, troubleshooting, spatial visualization and making independent decisions were cited as "new world" skills required for 21st-century manufacturing personnel. Additional related skills include attention to detail, personal flexibility, persistence and good communication[22]. The only "technical" skill listed was operating computers or computerized machinery. Certainly in the digital factory of the future, familiarity with computerization is the one central skill that pretty much every new collar worker needs. Technology is changing rapidly, and while the exact technologies may differ, Industry 4.0 is almost 100 percent digitally driven. Plus, digital job skills that we cannot imagine today will be required of the future workforce.

CHAPTER EIGHT
Fab Lab Hub's
New Collar Jobs Study

Partially funded by a contribution from the Verizon Foundation in 2016, I started research to look in more depth at the immediate worker needs U.S. manufacturers faced. Since founding Fab Lab Hub in 2010, I had many requests to participate in workforce development programs, especially from community colleges in the Fab Lab Network. Being steeped in market research protocols throughout my career, I instinctively wanted to develop curriculum, products and services that actually met the needs of manufacturers. In talking to 200 manufacturers ranging in size from large established multinationals to start-ups making a wide variety of high- and low-tech products in urban and rural areas across the country, I quickly developed a sense of the immediate new collar job skills needed today, as well as what might be expected from future workers.

Unequivocally, the No. 1 skill that 95 percent of employers interviewed want today from new collar workers is problem-solving ability. That was a bit of a surprise to me, as I had expected respondents to list the ability to use a particular software package or digital tool. But when you think about it, problem solving is at the heart of all activities in a factory and was central to my own hiring philosophy for many years. If a machine doesn't work and the manual doesn't solve the problem, what is a worker to do? Figure it out!

Tim Gornet, manager of operations at the University of Louisville's Rapid Prototyping Center, has told me that he wants interns and staff who are autodidacts. "We need people with a drive to learn, especially on their own. Our best people learn from failure and search for help themselves, either online or in vendor manuals. Of course, they need to know when to ask questions, but when they do seek help I know they've exhausted other means for solving the problem." Travis Steffens, founder and CEO of R Investments Inc. in Denver, Colo., sees problem-solving skills as being necessary for workers to learn and grow. Steffens told me that in his experience, "People have to feel contribution and purpose at work, and when it becomes their own idea, then the real magic happens. Our managers and supervisors consequently must learn to guide, rather than tell." One respondent commented, "Robots may be drilling the holes, but humans are still needed to solve problems."

My findings also fit with the TalentsLens report mentioned above, since the 21st-century skills they list represent aspects of problem solving. It is somewhat curious to note that problem solving has often been categorized as a "soft skill." I've always thought that without the soft skills — usually people skills — the "hard skills" would not succeed independently. In my mind, both types of skills have always been necessary and complementary for a worker to be successful in a high-tech company.

Lean manufacturing principles, one of the pillars of the GE Brilliant Factory, stress continuous improvement that is often initiated from workers' own intrinsic ability to see how processes are not functioning well. Companies that incorporate Lean into their culture encourage workers to find solutions to problems and motivate staff to participate in Lean programs. The New England Lean Consortium offers tours of member plants that allow the group to review Lean principles applied in the operation, and the visitors offer positive and negative feedback to the host. One tour stands out in my mind as a clear demonstration of how problem-solving staff members can become engaged workers. In 2016, we visited E.A. Dion Inc. a family-owned and operated jewelry manufacturing company that was founded in 1968 in Attleboro, Mass. We went into a production area where a man was doing a low-tech repetitive task. When he turned around to talk about the work in his department, it was clear he was energized and engaged in his work. After describing how his tasks fit into the full factory production, he talked with passion about the Lean contributions he and his team had made to the process. He was clearly proud to be valued by management and trusted to think, not just do something repetitively.

E.A. Dion's formal improvement process revolves around the Quick Kaizen Board, a visual method used in Lean programs to capture team members' ideas. Roland Dion, one of the owners, explained that employees were "given free rein to make changes as needed. With autonomy, people can modify space, travel time for stock or finished goods, and anything that improves the process and quality. Since it's an internal change, management doesn't have to get involved unless there is a big financial expense. We don't want to not include a good idea, and we trust our people. If additional resources are needed from different parts of the plant, then a group may form to complete the change."

Dion gets involved when it comes to motivating staff to write up their problem-solving ideas. "We must meet our corporate goal of 50 percent staff participation. If we meet our goal, then there is a performance reward." The reward calculation combines Quick Kaizen participation (a group method of solving problems) with quality and sales achievements and results in a cash gift card. In addition, the people who actively participate in Quick Kaizen also have the additional reward of participating in a drawing. An email goes to everyone sharing the Quick Kaizen board ideas, and ideas with photos are posted on a wall in a central location so that innovators get recognition. Roland points out, "We want everyone on the staff to emulate this Lean behavior, and recognition has helped expand the program in the plant. I borrowed the idea from AccuRounds (a precision manufacturer in Avon, Mass.), which also had success using decision-making autonomy with recognition of problem-solving initiative to improve quality and remove waste, the main goals of any Lean program … and employee engagement has been a wonderful benefit!"

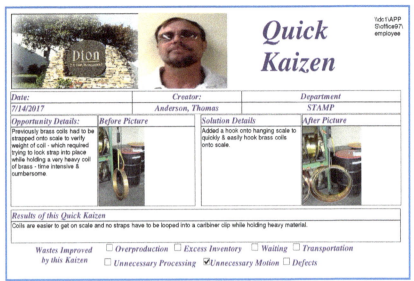

Date:	Creator:	Department
7/14/2017	Anderson, Thomas	STAMP

Contribution to a Quick Kaizen Board. Courtesy of E.A. Dion.

Innovation at Dion is central to the workplace through a creative Lean program designed to engage its people. Innovation does not have to mean inventing a new high-tech tool or creating a smartphone app. Innovation can involve changing patterns in workflow, reorganizing material distribution, revising paperwork requirements or restructuring a warehouse layout. If you think about it, Uber innovated by combining several existing technologies — GPS, smartphones, online payments, etc. — in a totally new way to better serve customers needing rides. It didn't invent any of the technologies but pulled them together to revamp an old, broken system into something new, efficient, cool and customer-centric.

New tools and technologies also require stronger problem-solving skills. Some 3D printer categories, for example, have inherent issues that require the end user to experiment until a solution is found. This is especially problematic in the under-$5,000 tabletop FDM, or fused deposition modeling, product range, which is often used in manufacturing for rapid prototyping. Since they were originally catering to the maker movement, most FDM 3D printer manufacturers assumed that the user enjoys getting the machine to print. But for industrial settings, all tools are a means to an end, enabling the worker to perform a task quickly and economically. While manuals and training from most vendors have improved, 3D printing is still not as solid as for a machine that has been in industrial use for decades. Often there is no historical knowledge within a company that another worker can depend on for help. In addition, manufacturing plants are devising new applications of these cutting-edge technologies with accompanying software and hardware modifications. It isn't possible for the machine's designer and builder to foresee custom applications; consequently, custom training materials do not exist for the end user.

Changes are happening at a faster pace, and the tools, technologies, processes and methodologies needed for new products and services today may become irrelevant in as little as a few days. Workers must be able to adapt to new situations and solve problems for which they were not trained. Another inspiring factory tour from the New England Lean Consortium clearly bears out this concept. Albany International in Rochester, N.H., was founded in 1895 and has reinvented itself for the 21st century. Originally it was a knitting mill that made custom-designed fabrics and machine belts essential to production in paper making and other process industries. The owners recognized that the paper market was declining and searched for a new application using the processes that had served them well over the years. Using profits from the stable fabric knitting business, Albany plowed R&D funds into trying new things. No material could be more modern than composites, and Albany's decades of industrial weaving experience combined with old-fashioned American ingenuity resulted in a sophisticated composite weaving process for the aerospace industry.

With a French partner, Safran, Albany designed 3D-woven resin transfer molding, or RTM, to weave thousands of high-tech fibers in a pattern that yields a lightweight yet strong part. Since Safran was producing the advanced LEAP engine with GE, the RTM process immediately found a market in manufacturing engine fan blades and fan cases. Adding automation and digitization, the time to weaving from design finalization is just a few days versus the months it took using analog processing. With higher fuel efficiency and reduced CO_2 emissions, the LEAP engine is in high demand. Albany predicts that production will grow from roughly 2,500 blades and 100 cases in 2015 to more than 40,000 blades and 2,000 fan cases per year by 2020. The RTM products for the LEAP engine could add as much as $200 million in annual sales for Albany by 2020. Other aerospace companies, including Rolls-Royce Engines and Gulfstream, are adding composite components from Albany to their military and commercial planes.

At the time of my visit, Albany's New Hampshire plant had about 1,000 workers, none of whom had been displaced by the addition of new technology to make the sophisticated new product line. Starting in 2007, the continually innovating company instituted a Lean/Six Sigma program that has helped transition workers to the new composites side of the business. The inherent employee-centric philosophy allowed the staff to participate in change, and problem-solving skills certainly came in handy when designing and implementing an entirely new production line.

Innovation is most often the outgrowth of problem solving, as evidenced by the adage, "Necessity is the mother of invention." While innovation has become a buzzword at many companies, those leaders who understand the sources of true innovation give employees the freedom to solve problems. Innovation, almost by definition, requires freedom: to think outside the box, defy the naysayers and try the impossible. Google has famously fostered a culture that attacks problems in a people-centric way. Eric Schmidt and Jonathan Rosenberg describe the process in their book, "How Google Works." Initiated by company co-founder Larry Page, the approach drew from his experience as a computer programmer rather than as a manager. When he saw a big problem, Page succinctly formulated the problem without mincing words and presented it to the entire company staff. One story has Page posting ads from the Google Adwords program in the community kitchen labeled in big letters, THESE ADS SUCK. He didn't place blame or attack people, but was rational and specific in his observation, and was confident that someone at Google would be challenged to step up to the plate with a solution. Jeff Howe describes a similar methodology used in multiple situations in his landmark book, "Crowdsourcing." More often than not, solutions to technical problems that Howe describes came from the least likely sources, including the finance and legal departments.

In my experience, giving staff this kind of freedom requires an intrinsic respect for the people in an organization. Most people come to work every day wanting to do a good job, and when they don't, it is most likely that I have not provided either the tools, processes, environment, clear goals or training for them to succeed. Occasionally someone is in the wrong job for his or her skillset, but with some experimentation we can usually correct the fit and both the worker and I are happier.

I make our production, financial and operational goals very clear, but usually I don't care exactly how a task is implemented as long as it is legal, ethical and doesn't harm anyone. It also seems to me that it is disrespectful to a person to not give them accurate performance feedback, both positive and negative. Respecting people enough to subjectively evaluate a situation usually results in them finding the solution to the problem themselves.

Vocabulary is key. Managers need to formulate problems around the situation, not the person, and natural problem solving will ensue. Asking "Why do you think the laser discharge tubes are cracking?" will foster innovation in a picosecond, while saying, "YOU are cracking discharge tubes because you're not following instructions" will just shut down a worker's interest in helping to solve the problem. I am always most interested in why a failure happened, because when we can get to the root of the problem, we have a chance of rectifying the underlying cause and (we hope) it won't be repeated. Finding out why a worker is not following instructions is a great place to start.

The second most mentioned skill for new collar workers was practical experience at working with their hands. This response reminded me of our own experience at Potomac Photonics in the late 1980s and early 1990s. Unlike Dr. Christensen, who had grown up on a sheep and cattle ranch in Colorado and worked in his family's construction business, most of our new engineering hires had never run a mill or lathe and didn't physically relate to our manufacturing processes. They did have strong computer skills, including programming, of course, but they could not go into our machine shop and create a fixture or a prototype with their own hands to turn their CAD designs to reality. When older engineers were kids with limited funds, they bought inoperable cars to fix up. That is not easy now, with computers running so much of today's automotive systems. As Potomac Photonics moved toward more contract service work, the operators and technicians we hired who

didn't need four-year engineering degrees to meet the job requirements came from backgrounds such as the military, community colleges or trade schools where they had gained practical, hands-on experience. This group of workers excelled, whereas young engineers had to learn hands-on skills on the job.

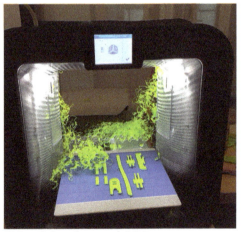

3D Print Failure. Courtesy of S. Boisvert.

Tim Gornet of the University of Louisville's Rapid Prototyping Center told me, "I look for interns and staff that have had hands-on hobbies, or who have worked on a farm, which here in Kentucky is easier to find than in other parts of the country. These kids have the kind of experience that directly translates to making things like 3D printers work in the lab." Interestingly, Gornet also mentioned that kids who had played sports understood failure, and of course, as Edison famously pointed out, engineering and innovation is essentially moving forward through a series of failures until a viable solution is found.

Travis Steffens, of R Investments Inc., says that while new technology is revolutionizing the building trades, hands-on abilities are still key for new hires at his company. The concept of play also fits into these criteria. In recent years, research has emerged that validates how play creates neural pathways to creative thinking, and yes, problem solving. Psychiatrist Stuart Brown in his book, "Play: How it Shapes the Brain, Opens the Imagination, and Invigorates the Soul," states unequivocally that, "Play lies at the core of creativity and innovation." In fact, when I talked with colleagues at the Jet Propulsion Laboratory in Pasadena, Calif., during my research, they recalled that they had found a correlation between successful staff and a childhood of hands-on activities and play. Now job interview questions at JPL include probing what the human resources department labels "youthful projects and play" to find the best candidates for problem-solving capabilities on the job.

Coming in third in the manufacturers survey of needed skills was what I would categorize as digital skills: the ability to read and modify CAD files, design from scratch in CAD, access information via the internet on smart devices such as tablets, utilize sophisticated software to monitor sensors from the IoT and analyze the resulting data, as well as some computer programming. I am a firm believer that all digital fabrication is only as good as the CAD design on which it is built. In my experience at Potomac Photonics, a poor or unclear design file from customers was the most frequent challenge to our ability to quickly process a part. Potomac Photonics' Mike Adelstein agrees and has told me that he believes all students should learn CAD in school. Operators need to be able to read a CAD file to plan a processing job around the designated material, shapes, thicknesses and other parameters set out in the design.

With 3D printing's potential future application in everyday life, CAD is most likely to become even more important for future generations. It's comparable to the number of college-track high-school students who never learned to touch type and now "hunt and peck" on the computer keyboards that seem to rule the workplace. Fortunately, many kids today are taken with the sandbox video game Minecraft, which is a natural progression to CAD, since virtual worlds are built using 3D building blocks. For our youngest students, I usually recommend starting with Minecraft when introducing 3D printing, as there are many hacks that allow for direct file transfer to the printer. Seeing a physical representation of a Minecraft world enhances the child's learning experience.

One of the study's respondents pointed out that an operator's ability to optimize a CAD design so that the process was more efficient directly affected his company's bottom line. Good designs reduce processing time and material waste while improving quality parameters. Combined with problem-solving skills, CAD ability greatly enhances the build process, improving the finished part. Operators and technicians also often need to design custom fixtures for processing a part, making CAD design an essential skill for operators, especially since fixturing is becoming a frequent application of 3D printing.

While generative design is on the horizon, today most manufacturing companies still use CAD to drive digital fabrication machines. CAD has become far more intuitive, and for digital natives, the concepts are usually easy to pick up. At Potomac Photonics, Mike Adelstein looks to local colleges for new hires and has found that students coming out of the Maryland Institute College of Art have design capabiltiies that give them an edge over other job candidates. Program skills cited by the survey respondents ranged from AutoCAD, which is more suited to laser or CNC processing, to Autodesk Fusion 360, Inventor and Maya for 3D printing design applications. Solidworks, Rhino and SketchFAB were also mentioned as frequently used software.

Programming embedded-device controllers is another computer skill that fell into this category. A factory's interconnectivity is specific to its configuration of sensors, computers, manufacturing tools, security protocols and applications that are integrated into a complete system, requiring custom programming. Languages used for programming embedded systems include C, C++, Java and Python, all of which are listed in its 2017 Top 10 programming languages by IEEE, the Institute of Electrical and Electronic Engineers. It is interesting that Los Alamos National Laboratory mentioned needing workers who could program Arduinos, the open-source microcontrollers popular in the maker movement that use an integrated development environment (IDE) written in Java. The Arduino IDE supports C++, making it quite versatile.

The ability to mine and analyze data coming from the Internet of Things is another new skill showing up on the factory floor. Standard programming languages such as SQL, which was originally invented at IBM for storing, manipulating and retrieving information in databases, have found important applications in manufacturing. Proprietary software is now available from IBM, SAP, HP, Oracle and other companies, many offering cloud-based solutions. While building databases requires higher-level education, jobs for junior data analysts using these tools often require less than a four-year degree. I'm also seeing an uptick in the sale of mainframe computers, with the popularity of the cloud. Technicians to install and service these machines are consequently needed to keep them running.

Simply being able to use custom software is important in a wide range of jobs. R Investments, mentioned earlier, is a leader in next-generation building construction processes that has developed specialized software balancing labor, materials, funding and time. Quality control staff and supervisors on projects use the company's custom software, Sidewinder, to track current positions within a project. Adding dollar values to each element allows the company to track exactly where it stands at any point in the production process. IT manager Dusten Hale talked about how the Sidewinder software development team examined how many variables could be removed to streamline processes: "The approach is generally how simple can we make it for the end user. However, there is a certain level of expectation for workers in today's digital era for following the software flow, which is key to our company's success." Pre-fabrication in large-scale projects has been a part of construction for the past few decades, led by China's Broad Sustainable Building Co. procedure for building skyscrapers in a fraction of the usual construction time. Assembly is at the root of the change, and workers must need to know how to read a digital assembly diagram rather than swing a hammer. With resulting cost savings, Broad has gotten worldwide attention and plans to license its construction designs and technology to other companies.

I expected mathematics to be a desired skill in today's manufacturing processes, but manufacturers most often mentioned needing operators and technicians who possess solid ability in arithmetic. New hires seem to have problems with basic concepts such as converting fractions to decimals or vice versa. The need for these skills is so great that CNC milling machine manufacturer Forest Scientific has created a math poster for its customers to aid workers on the factory floor. Many manufacturers also need workers to be able to move freely to and from metric and English units of measure.

Moving to mathematics, the most cited areas were geometry, trigonometry and basic algebra. Many people will be happy to note that advanced math such as differential equations are not needed for this level of work. Geometry, of course, is a pretty obvious choice since we are dealing with fabrication of physical objects in space. In this same area, measurement skills are key, particularly for quality control. The Los Alamos National Laboratory cited a need for more training in me-

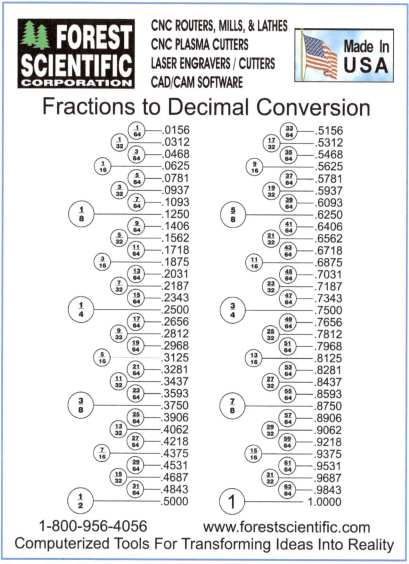

Courtesy of Forest Scientific Corp.

trology, the science of measurement, in order for workers to accurately measure units in practice and then trace them to reference standards. Metrology skills ensure meeting specifications for advanced products, as well as calibrating tools.

A few companies, such as Optomec, a pioneer in 3D printed electronics with operations in Albuquerque, N.M., and St. Paul, Minn., need workers who can understand machine tool paths. Designing in CAD is an essential skill, but translating the file to G-code actually instructs the machine on using the file to make a part. The toolpath, however, is more complex than the drill bit or laser cutting a pattern with the least amount of extraneous tool movement. Factors such as stress, sharp corners and cut entry need to be taken into account when determining an optimal toolpath. Benefits besides faster processing speeds include a better surface finish and less tool wear, in the case of mechanical CNC. Not surprisingly, toolpath is also an important factor in successful 3D printing. Advanced users will often look at toolpath before starting to print to optimize parameters in the printer settings for more robust parts and, often, time savings.

It is interesting to observe that the 200 manufacturers interviewed are looking for new collar workers with the foundational skills that are an underlying job requirement for any number of tasks. While the mainstream media abounds with stories of unemployed blue collar workers taking a specific course only to find that the job they trained for is obsolete, research shows that new collar workers demonstrating competency in broad skills are in high demand today. As technology rapidly changes, we may not have even invented the tools that will be on the factory floor in the next few years.

The Fab Lab Hub study also looked at next-generation manufacturing skills that are just emerging and are being introduced into production settings at the most progressive manufacturing companies.

Additive manufacturing is starting to exhibit enough reliability that it has drawn substantial investment from advanced manufacturers. Consequently, the ability to operate 3D printing tools is a new collar skill showing up in job postings. Today, over 1,000 open jobs on each of the major hiring sites list 3D printing skills as being required for applicants. At the 2016 RAPID conference where HP entered the additive manufacturing, or AM, equipment market by offering a new production 3D printer, I most often heard, "I'd buy that new HP machine, but who (at my plant) would run it"?

Lack of trained staff has been targeted by many in the industry as a key barrier to AM technology adoption. Ed Tackett, director of education programs at the UL Additive Manufacturing Competency Center at the University of Louisville, reported data to support my empirical findings at the 2017 Formlabs Digital Factory conference. Surveying over 1,700 manufacturers, he found that 75.7 percent of the respondents have found that a lack of skilled AM professionals has affected their ability to adopt or expand into additive manufacturing.

Tackett sees that the rapid adoption rate of 3D printing is now outpacing the number of operators, technicians and engineers being trained in the field. Although his research is still in progress as of this writing, he also has received interesting feedback from manufacturers regarding the subjects they felt workers needed experience with to be successful in additive manufacturing. Topping the list, 81.1 percent of respondents said that material science understanding was their most important skill requirement for 3D printing. Not surprisingly, 62.2 percent of the respondents said design was essential for AM workers, and tied with the same percentage were those who rated post-processing as essential. Often called the "dirty little secret of 3D printing," post-processing is often complicated and destroys the myth that all parts come out of the printer ready to be used. Other skills mentioned ranged from topology optimization to lightweighting, with safety getting a low response rate of just 35.1 percent. Since metal 3D printers use laser sources that generate heat, flammable metal powders can be a safety issue if not handled properly, so safety perhaps should be a bit higher in importance.

I've observed several companies that decided to delve into 3D printing and added its care and feeding to the responsibilities of someone in the IT department who had built a "home" device. Invariably

I'm asked during a visit to provide some help with poor print results, and I quickly realize that the company wrongly assumed that 3D printers were akin to a 2D paper printer. Keeping AM machines up and running requires more attention than an employee with other full-time duties can spare. My response to companies that ask for suggestions on "better" 3D printers is to first try hiring a dedicated intern or part-time 3D printing specialist before determining if their 3D printer choice was right for their application. More and more companies are realizing that adding 3D printing to their operation is no small feat and have started finding a dedicated operator or tech to go with the equipment purchase.

Functional prototype 3D-printed at Fab Lab Hub on the MakerBot Replicator+ requires no assembly and reduces parts count from four to one. Courtesy of P. Boisvert.

Design for manufacturability became an important concept in CAD, since beautiful designs often could not be successfully fabricated. Taking this concept a step further, design for 3D printing is an important next-generation new collar job skill. 3D printing can create previously unimagined parts, so transferring a part directly from 2D to 3D processing does not take advantage of additive manufacturing's unique properties. It reminds me of the early days of website design. The first websites looked like print ads, but as designers took advantage of the web's unique capabilities, the interfaces were seamless and interactive features took center stage. As additive expands, designers are needed who can make the same transition as happened in website design and generate totally new concepts that take advantage of the complex geometries and other features now available to them through 3D printing.

The skills that new collar workers need for additive manufacturing are quite broad, drawing from programming, materials science, mechanics, measurement, post-processing and design. In addition, metal 3D printing has additional requirements for understanding metallurgy, gas flow and lasers.

Implications for Workforce Training

Our research was certainly illuminating and builds a strong case for even more aggressive education reform. As one of the manufacturers told me in an interview, "Good engineers are a dime a dozen," supporting my own observations that engineering education in the 21st century is strong. Not so for operators and technicians. New collar jobs that bridge the blue collar and engineering workforce are where the biggest opportunities lie if the middle class is going to make a resurgence. But it will take concerted effort for education systems to catch up to new collar job training demand. The two areas that must urgently be examined for investment are problem-based learning and apprenticeships.

CHAPTER NINE
The Case for Problem-Based Learning

Benjamin Franklin famously said, "Tell me, and I forget. Teach me, and I remember. Involve me, and I learn." Problem-based learning has been at the forefront of education initiatives in the past few years but it is really not new. The foundational methodology of critical thinking and learning by doing was used by the ancient philosophers in China, Japan, India and Greece, and educational theorists like John Dewey in the United States and Jean Piaget in Switzerland advocated for experiential learning during the 20th century. For decades problem sets have been the teaching method of choice at technical universities, especially the Massachusetts Institute of Technology. Rather than 100 percent teacher-led learning, the students engage in finding answers themselves. MIT likes to say that it trains students in every major to be the world's problem solvers. Although collaboration with other students and help from teaching staff is allowed, the work that is turned in is expected to be an original solution to the problem.

In watching Dr. Christensen solve tough engineering problems at Potomac Photonics, it was clear to me that he had a strong problem-solving methodology, most likely honed at MIT where he completed his master's degree and at the University of California, Berkeley, where he earned his Ph.D., both in electrical engineering. He confirmed that "over and over again I've used the approaches I learned through problem

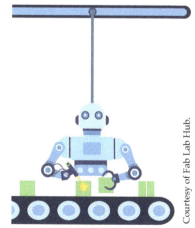

Courtesy of Fab Lab Hub.

sets to find useful approximate solutions to engineering problems in optics, heat flow, mechanics, electromagnetics and similar areas" that were needed in our laser manufacturing and laser micromachining business.

Dr. Christensen continued, "Most of the engineering, math and physics courses throughout graduate school used problem sets. They were a lot of work, but they were a very important part of the learning process. I think the problem sets were a bridge between classroom lectures and the real world. It's easy to walk out of a lecture and think you understand something and a few days or weeks later find that you don't really know enough to do anything useful. Problem sets typically took real-world problems that would be very difficult to solve exactly, simplified them by making useful approximations and then required a solution of the simpler approximate problem. Sometimes, the approximation was still difficult to solve. Through this approach, we learned how to make useful approximations, and we also had to dig deep into the basic principles to solve the approximate problem. Spending hours on problems sets for a particular course also had the benefit of embedding the knowledge much deeper into your brain and helped development of an intuitive understanding of the processes involved."

Problem sets are quite time-consuming and can be burdensome for technical majors carrying a heavy course load. Dr. Christensen reflected, "Perhaps, without the time required by problem sets, I might have been able to take more courses or have time for other educational experiences. I guess the trade-off is narrower and deeper versus broader and shallower, and there are arguments to be made on both sides." In my early experience at Potomac Photonics it was Dr. Christensen's ability to delve into complex problems and solve them quickly and elegantly that differentiated our company from our competitors.

Modern-day Problem Based Learning, or PBL, is a methodology involving defined protocols with origins in training medical school students in diagnostics. Harold Barrows was a professor and physician with a specialty in neurology who in 1971 joined the faculty of the newly formed Medical School at McMaster University in Hamilton, Ontario, Canada. He almost immediately recognized a disconnect between the facts medical students were required to memorize and the work that actually happens when diagnosing patients. Since the McMaster curriculum was just being finalized, Barrows had significant input into the way students were to be trained at the new institution. Drawing from his work in clinical reasoning, Barrows argued that training should mimic the actual process used by experienced doctors in everyday practice. His landmark paper, "An Investigation of Diagnostic Problem Solving," appeared in *Mathematical Biosciences* in 1972 and problem-pased learning as we know it today was born. The pedagogical model spread to medical schools in Australia, the Netherlands and New Mexico in the United States. In recent years, PBL has become a hot topic for K-12 educational institutions where change in teaching methods is being actively explored to improve learning experiences. The justification is often that education in STEM and STEAM subjects must be upgraded to educate the worker of the future. If the responses to our skills survey were any indication, PBL is a perfect fit in today's workforce training.

There are many misconceptions about PBL, and the most prevalent is that it just involves "doing projects." In practice, PBL in formal educational settings is a structured learning environment involving small groups of students who work in teams. The instructor is a facilitator who guides the students to analyze a situation and define the problem, plan the overall project, implement tasks and review the outcomes. Teachers are helping the students in the path to solving a problem rather than disseminating facts or data. The teacher must be especially active in formulating the problems, for as many people say, accurately identifying the problem is the most challenging element of all problem solving.

According to the Buck Institute for Education (BIE), which provides training and materials to teachers interested in applying PBL in their classrooms, essential PBL design elements must be integrated into the program in order for it to be completely successful. These include:

• Key Knowledge, Understanding, and Success Skills

PBL is not free-form for the student. The teacher designs projects to cover the content that is required by the school's curriculum and to meet state and national standards. For example, if geometry is the topic, the project may involve solving a problem related to architecture for solar homes. Other skills such as collaboration and teamwork might also be nurtured in the project.

• Challenging Problem or Question

PBL projects are always framed by a problem to solve that is challenging but that doesn't inappropriately exceed the knowledge level of the students. The problem also captures the students' imaginations, stimulating them to engage in the process.

• Sustained Inquiry

PBL is a rigorous, longer-term process of questioning, finding appropriate resources and then applying data to the problem. Unlike a term paper, the work is more interactive and may involve interviews with experts, as well as testing design concepts in the lab. The process is iterative: find answers, test, refine.

• Authenticity

Thinking back to the importance of social impact for millennials, solving real-world problems that have meaning to the students is a key element in designing the project.

• Student Voice and Choice

Ownership of the project will give the students motivation to solve the problem at hand. It is a special skill to guide a student to achieve the results we need to learn while also allowing for freedom to choose specific aspects of the project.

• Reflection, Critique and Revision

Drawing from education reformer John Dewey's insistence that, "We do not learn from experience. We learn from reflecting on experience," PBL encourages critical analysis of the process and outcomes experienced by students, so that everyone involved might learn and move forward to deeper understanding.

• Public Product

The result might be an actual product, but more often than not it is the solution to a problem. By sharing with parents, school, friends and the community in a public way such as an expo, the students are given the real-world practice of presenting their work and stakeholders begin to see what happens in PBL.

I was first introduced to PBL by Rich Lehrer, a veteran teacher who is a BIE national faculty member. While consulting for the Enable Community Foundation a few years ago, I learned about his work on 3D printing prosthetics with his middle-school students in Massachusetts. The project was driven by his personal experience of having a young son born without fully developed fingers on one hand. I invited Lehrer and his students to present their work at Fab Lab Hub's annual meeting, DigiFabCon. It was astonishing to see how these young people took their project so seriously and had produced such sophisticated 3D-printed prosthetics. Lehrer is adamant that authentic projects that affect lives is the key to engaging students. I have seen how the stories that come from authentic projects garner the attention of funders and supporters, making win-win propositions.

Reporting in *The Interdisciplinary Journal of Problem-Based Learning*

Max Lehrer demonstrates his prosthetic hand 3D-printed by his Dad, Rich, and students at the school where he uses PBL. Courtesy of Rich Lehrer.

and other academic publications, researchers from leading education institutions have found statistical support for the PBL methodology. In general, PBL appears to be most effective for long-term retention of information and specific skill development while engaging both students and teachers, and instilling a sense of accomplishment. These areas of achievement indicate that true, deep-seated learning is happening, at least by Benjamin Franklin's definition. PBL was not as effective in short-term information retention, which, of course, is the basis of current standardized testing, begging the question, "Are we testing for the best learning outcomes?"

In informal education settings such as maker spaces and fab labs, PBL activities vary widely. Some programs in schools or libraries offer structured PBL classes. Membership-based programs in community centers tend to foster self-directed projects that interest makers. Digital fabrication equipment manufacturers are realizing the importance of helping over-worked teachers with little spare time for new learning modalities.

Roland DGA, a printer supplier, now makes available an online project-based guide for customers to learn how to operate their vinyl cutters and 3D milling machines, as well as have a head start with ready-made lesson plans for their classes. Roland's business development manager, Adam Sebran, who started the initiative, said, "So many teachers find the online PBL resources very, very helpful. They say that we're helping them do their job, which is gratifying." In all scenarios, problems are being solved in order to meet a goal, be it building a competition winning robot or creating mom's birthday present. Regardless of the problem-solving methodology being applied, everyone is working with their hands and learning fundamental fabrication principles.

MC2 STEM High School in Cleveland, Ohio, is in one of the most socio-economically challenged school districts in the nation. When the school opened in 2008, the district's average ACT test score was 16, a full four points below the workforce readiness national goal, and high-school graduation rates were at 54 percent. MC2 features a curriculum heavily steeped in problem-solving and critical-thinking activities involving hands-on creation in the fab lab. Not just relegated to STEM subjects, the entire curriculum uses digital fabrication tools to create a true STEAM program. Not only have standardized test scores in science and math increased, in one year's time, reading scores improved from the 38th to the 75th percentile. There are no enrollment criteria, so this public-private partnership school is not for already elite learners, yet almost 100 percent of the student body has graduated since the school's opening. Most interesting for manufacturing are the internships, especially at GE Lighting, where one of the campuses is located. One of the anecdotal success stories reported in the national news features MC2 graduate David Boone, whose family was driven from their inner-city home by gangs. Living on the street and getting mostly Cs and Ds in school, Boone was guided by caring adults to MC2. The school challenged his innate intelligence and curiosity, allowing him to win a full scholarship to Harvard to study engineering. He eventually switched his major to computer science and is now a data analyst for Microsoft in Seattle.

Both empirical evidence and structured research results support using PBL at The Hardesty Center for Fab Lab Tulsa in Tulsa, Okla. As part of its mission, Fab Lab Tulsa provides educational opportunities for the Kendall-Whittier neighborhood where it is located. The Fab Lab interacts with and provides additional programming for schools in the neighborhood through informal STEM education activities such as workshops, classes, camps and challenges. It also organizes a citywide mini-Maker Faire. Executive Director Nathan Pritchett recognized the need for a program specific to middle-school students. This age group is old enough to use design software and be safe in the fab lab, so they were ideal candidates for learning STEM through digital fabrication. This also encouraged interest in STEM careers, which is best accomplished before students enter high school. Pritchett explains that he and the fab lab manager beta tested the program, seeing approximately 800 students. Knowing he was headed in the right direction, he secured funding and hired an education director. But as is often the case with grants, Fab Lab Tulsa's program had to show impact within one year or the funding was lost. "We had lots of anecdotal evidence of impact," Pritchett recalled. "For example, we worked with a school that had a chronic attendance issue, but each week that the fab lab was at the school 100 percent of the students showed up."

Showing impact is not an unusual demand. Most philanthropic organizations today require that recipients demonstrate that contributions are being put to good use, and future funding hinges on demonstrable results. Pritchett realized that he had to clearly show impact because of the philanthropic community's mindset, so he set about to measure the effectiveness of the education initiatives. Fab Lab Tulsa is strategically situated close to the University of Oklahoma local campus where Pritchett was familiar with the work of Dr. Chan Hellman. In addition to his appointment as associate dean of the College of Arts and Sciences, Dr. Hellman is the founding director of The Center of Applied Research for Nonprofit Organizations, which trains graduate students to conduct outcome assessments. The center's work was a perfect fit for the research needed by Fab Lab Tulsa. Dr. Hellman agreed to take it on for several reasons. "In looking at the literature, there was clearly a need for study in the area," said Dr. Hellman, "Plus, the National Science Foundation and the White House both commented on the need to increase student self-efficacy. So we were able to tie the research to priorities of these two institutions. I felt we'd be meeting the national agenda with this study, as well as helping Fab Lab Tulsa locally."

Dr. Hellman and his graduate students' guiding principle is that nonprofits are pathways of hope. He explains, "We have found that future expectation of success among a study's participants has a high correlation with hope — especially for female participants. But to be hopeful, individuals must have motivation along with pathways. Nonprofits sometimes provide one or the other, but Fab Lab Tulsa could provide both elements, increasing the student's chances of success. One might ask, 'Why did we measure self-efficacy?' and I'll tell you, one of single best predictors of academic achievement is self-efficacy. Self-efficacy equals the self-confidence that a child can attain goals that are under his or her control. With STEM the real question is, do they feel like they can control the outcomes? Of course, there is always the context of one's environment. If there is no STEM program at school, then aptitude doesn't matter, so we don't measure it in that way. I am most interested in the impact and outcomes nonprofits can have on our communities."

To participate in the study, students had to meet clearly defined requirements, such as minimal attendance at the weekly program. From a large pool of middle-school students, 250 were in the final study, participating in both the pre-test and post-test assessment. Of these,

46 percent were girls, and it was a diverse group, with 80 percent of the students from racial minorities. Before and after the STEM instruction at Fab Lab Tulsa, students were asked to agree or disagree with statements such as, "I am comfortable using technology to design or make things." Nicholas Dubriwny, who was a graduate student with Dr. Hellman at the time, compiled and analyzed the data using rigorous statistical methods. The results demonstrated a statistically significant increase in self-efficacy from 23.68 to 24.23 mean scores after participating in the program. There was also a slight increase in the students' attitude toward STEM, but it was not statistically significant. Although the study started out as what Nathan Pritchett calls "self-preservation," Dr. Hellman convinced Fab Lab Tulsa that the report should be submitted to a peer-reviewed journal. *The Journal of Stem Education* was chosen, as it is an open publication with free internet access, allowing other fab labs, educational institutions and maker spaces to use the data and procedures from the paper.

Overall it seems that PBL is turning teaching away from an assembly-line approach back to an individualized process where teachers and students engage in a two-way interaction. The methodology has entered both formal and informal teaching situations, demonstrating a marked increase in actual learning. Still, assessment and standardized testing needs to catch up and change along with it. Many school districts and colleges are reevaluating their policies and practices, along with the system's entire philosophical underpinnings. But change is slow, especially on this scale. At least the pendulum has started to swing and pockets of change are coming to light to inspire everyone in the trenches. For anyone seeking a new collar job, this is important news. PBL in STEM is a natural choice for training operators and technicians for next generation manufacturing jobs, equipping the high-tech workforce for Industry 4.0.

CHAPTER TEN
Apprenticeships and Internships

Perhaps the purest form of PBL is the apprenticeship that has its roots in the Middle Age trade guilds. To learn a trade in the days before we had high schools or universities, many children between the ages of 10 and 15 were sent to live with a master for as many as seven to 10 years to gain first-hand experience. Without doubt, the problems that an apprentice may have faced were authentic, as they were on-the-job issues that are encountered in everyday work. But times changed and the codification of trade practices was demanded throughout Europe, and that could not be accomplished one-on-one. The guilds actually spawned some of the world's most prestigious universities, including the University of Oxford, founded in the United Kingdom around 1096.

Modern apprenticeship programs exist and even thrive in some countries. Many people believe that Germany leads Europe in manufacturing due to its long history of apprenticeships, providing industry with a highly skilled workforce. Formal apprenticeships are offered in everything from harpsichord building to baking, plumbing to banking and CNC machining to biological laboratory assisting. The government estimates that 50 percent to 60 percent of Germany's young people participate in an apprenticeship program that averages three years in length. In the United States, it is closer to 5 percent of a population that is about four times larger than Germany's. Most of the 505,000 American apprentices fill 144,583 slots in construction and 95,000 places in the military. In 2016, there were only 14,422 manufacturing apprentices in U.S. Department of Labor-registered programs.

The German model is called the Dual Education System because activities are a combination of classes in a vocational school and on-the-job training. By working simultaneously while learning theory, the student can instantly apply knowledge, in turn deepening meaning. In recent years, there has been a slight decline in students applying for apprenticeships. This recent phenomenon is perhaps due to American influence promoting four-year degrees. But if John Deere in Mannheim, Germany, is any indication, each year there are about 3,100 qualified applicants for 60 apprenticeship openings. Any American company would be happy with that, if only for the interest it demonstrates in manufacturing. The Dual Education System is a true partnership between vocational schools and industry. As discussed earlier in the project-based learning section, best results are seen when students undertake authentic projects.

The fact that German manufacturers take an active role in determining the education curriculum that fits their individual factory needs ensures that real-world problems are addressed in the student's learning experience.

Internships require a substantial investment from industry partners. Depending on the field of study and location in Germany, a company can spend between $25,000 and $80,000 per apprentice. In the United States, it is estimated that German-style apprenticeships would cost substantially more, partly because in Germany the government pays for the education component.

A few European companies have created German-style apprenticeships in the locations where they have U.S. operations and were struggling to find competent manufacturing workers. Julius Blum GmbH spearheaded one of the most notable dual education programs in 1995 in the Charlotte, N.C., region. The four-year program recruits high-school juniors and seniors to learn the skills needed as tool and die makers, machinists and electricians. Other companies joined in as industry partners, including Timken, Ameritech, Pfaff Molds, Siemens, Chiron and Sarstedt. American companies might balk at footing the bill for apprenticeship programs, but manufacturers such as Blum report high retention rates of as much as 80 percent for trainees. As any employer will attest, finding and training new talent is much more expensive than retaining trained staff.

In a compelling article in *The Atlantic*, journalist Tamar Jacoby documented a visit to Germany to research apprenticeships. She wrote: "Our group heard the same thing in plant after plant: We're teaching more than skills. 'In the future, there will be robots to turn the screws,' one educator told us. 'We don't need workers for that. What we need are people who can solve problems — skilled, thoughtful, self-reliant employees who understand the company's goals and methods and can improvise when things go wrong or when they see an opportunity to make something work better." Clearly, apprenticeships combined with hands-on project-based learning can help reach employers' goals of finding new collar workers who can solve problems.

Internships are quite different from apprenticeships. Perhaps most striking is the time commitment. While the average apprenticeship in the United States lasts at least one year and more likely two to three years, internships are usually completed in a semester or as a summer project. Internships may or may not be paid, although the Department of Labor monitors unpaid programs to ensure that education is the goal, not free labor for the employer. Internships are most common as part of the college experience, while apprenticeships may start earlier in high school. Apprenticeships, at least in the European dual education model, are connected to a simultaneous formal education experience, usually at a vocational school or community college. Apprenticeships usually result in a full-time job, partially due to the industry partner's financial investment in the endeavor. Although apprenticeships are more intense than internships, the latter provide an introduction to an industry, practical experience and exposure to topics such as quality control that are not covered in the classroom. And in both cases the student has an opportunity to try a job and see what it's really like in day-to-day work that is often not as glamorous as the recruitment ads make it seem.

Drawing students from Fab Lab Baltimore at the Community College of Baltimore County, the University of Maryland Baltimore County and the Maryland Institute College of Art, Potomac Photonics initiated an active paid internship program to develop a digital fabrication jobs pipeline. Mike Adelstein has said that the students coming from these schools for internships as CAD designers and laser, CNC, and 3D printer operators demonstrate stronger skills than previous job applicants who were not exposed to these specialized training programs. Most of the interns have full-time jobs waiting for them at Potomac Photonics, and the Baltimore community interaction this has generated is particularly gratifying.

PART THREE

Innovative Training Programs

Riding the bus in Cambridge, Mass., is unlike using public transportation anywhere else. I routinely find myself sitting next to university professors from Harvard, Boston University and MIT, as well as bright high-school and college students. I once heard a small group of recently graduated high-school students discussing their future plans. A few had been accepted to elite schools and planned to pursue technical degrees, but most interesting were two young men who were going to skip college, at least for now. Each of them had been offered six-figure salaries to start work immediately as computer programmers. "Why spend money on an education that doesn't interest me?" asked one. "I'll be getting paid to do what I love and I can always take classes down the road to expand my skills into new areas." These autodidacts are following in the footsteps of Silicon Valley heroes who skipped traditional higher education to go on and make fortunes.

Educators realize that to capture the imaginations of young people, the old model must change. Beyond pedagogical elements such as project-based learning and apprenticeships that are being incorporated into traditional workforce training programs, I am seeing totally new, innovative types of training for new collar jobs. The next part of this book describes programs that stand out particularly because they transform old notions of what constitutes an education into modern-day answers that address 21st-century manufacturing needs.

CHAPTER ELEVEN
Fab Lab and
Makerspace Programs

The maker movement brings with it exposure to the two top skills that 21st-century manufacturing requires: problem solving and hands-on experience. Serving the needs of the DIY (do it yourself) and DIWO (do it with others) crowd, *Make Magazine* and open-source conferences promoted club-type organizations that offer self-proclaimed "geeks and nerds" a place to make things, collaborate and socialize. Peer-to-peer experimentation with 3D printing, laser cutting, CNC machining, digital sewing and a myriad of other tools may be supplemented in a maker space by more formal classes and workshops that are often used to raise funds for software, tools and materials. An internal study, conducted several years ago by Open Works in Baltimore, found that members were predominately middle-aged white men, although that is changing as more young people and women are encouraged to join maker spaces. I actually just heard about a maker space program from a colleague who teaches women how to use CNC and welding tools to make a wine rack. After each class the ladies shed their safety gear and share a glass of wine and the camaraderie of other female makers.

Fab labs, on the other hand, are an outgrowth of the Center for Bits and Atoms at MIT. Around the turn of the last century, Professor Neil Gershenfeld received funding from the National Science Foundation to found CBA, and community outreach was part of the grant requirements. Dr. Gershenfeld created a course entitled, "How to Make (almost) Anything," which he taught at MIT and in a local community center. He expected it to appeal mostly to the engineering community, but a wide range of people from varying backgrounds took the course. Most surprising, perhaps, were the ingenious projects they created that answered real-world problems. The "sheet removal pulley" alarm clock is one of my favorites, created by a student who didn't like to get out of bed for class but was forced to get up when the covers were removed by an electro-mechanical alarm. Word of the cool new class spread, and the program exploded. There are now over 1,200 fab labs or digital FABrication LABoratories in more than 80 countries around the world, and Dr. Gershenfeld is still teaching his landmark course at MIT and through FabAcademy. In 2009, the Fab Foundation was born to help support the Fab Lab Network and to help bring new fab labs online. Director Sherry Lassiter says time and again that the Fab Lab Network is so special because of its community of dedicated fabricators thinking creatively and bringing ideas to life via the tools of digital fabrication and, most important, sharing them with each other.

Fab labs are quite similar to maker spaces in that they are typically open-source-oriented, provide access to a range of tools that a participant would not have at home and foster collaboration among people internally. However, fab labs have a bit more structure than a maker space. Although CBA owns none of the fab labs, and communities with widely diverse aspirations drive the initiation of local fab labs, there is a powerful sense of collaboration among fab labs. Organizations as different as K-12 school systems, universities, community colleges, innovation centers, museums, libraries and community groups have started fab labs, but there is a powerful sense that they operate as an informal network to help each other and advance digital fabrication concepts. To be approved as part of the Fab Lab Network, a maker space must have five types of digital fabrication tools: laser cutting and marking, CNC machining, 3D printing, vinyl cutting and microelectronics, all tied together with CAD design. The fab lab must also demonstrate community interaction, making the tools available to local groups from outside the sponsoring organization. Fab labs also participate in FabAcademy, which offers the "How to Make (almost) Anything" course through video conferencing lectures by Dr. Gershenfeld and hands-on projects

Group discussion at DigiFabCon 2017 in MIT Media Lab. Courtesy of Stan Rowin.

in the local host lab with fab gurus. Graduation from the intensive 20-week courses occurs at the annual gathering of the entire network.

Dr. Gershenfeld likes to say, "The power of digital fabrication is social, not technical," and fab labs continually demonstrate social impact in education, workforce training, entrepreneurship, start-up creation and community building. More than just providing instruction for the technical side of the machines and processes, fab labs instill participants with the ability to solve problems. The method is quite like how engineers are trained in the scientific method: Try something, fail, learn from the experience, try something different based on the new knowledge and see if it works. Fab labs are a safe place to fail, for it is in failure that we advance knowledge. Dr. Christensen at Potomac Photonics says, "We don't know what we don't know and it is through quick, inexpensive experimentation to try ideas that we learn the heart of the issue and can determine how to move forward toward solving a problem."

Problem solving in the fab lab often is an outgrowth of a real issue that is facing the individual or the local community. There are many inspiring stories of a fab lab having social impact; here are some of their stories.

Rural Indian Fab Lab Fosters Entrepreneurship

The first lab outside the United States was in rural India. After achieving success in business and engineering at multinational Unilever, the late Dr. S.S. Kalbag returned to his roots in rural India because he was concerned about the school drop-out rate among the locals. He started the Vigyan Ashram in the drought-prone village of Pabal to see what he could do to improve education for the community. When he met Neil Gershenfeld, he knew that a fab lab would inspire his students, and the ability to build useful things in the lab helped achieve his goals. One day, a student came to the ashram upset because the family bull had died, a disaster for a poor farmer who depended on animal power to work the land. The other students put their heads together, employed parts from a discarded motorcycle in the fab lab, and built a mechanical bull. No, not like the featured entertainment in a Texas saloon, but a mechanical version of the deceased bull — basically, a small tractor. The student immediately put the "Mech Bull" to work, and word spread to neighboring farms. A John Deere tractor at that time cost $40,000, which was prohibitive for poor Indian farmers. But the students discovered they could sell the Mech Bull for a fraction of the cost of an American tractor, and a business was born. Since then, the Vigyan Ashram Fab Lab has worked with the local farmers to find solutions to a wide variety of agricultural problems including animal husbandry, water sanitation and food preservation.

Connecting the World with Digital Fabrication

Like any modern inner city, Detroit has a wealth of issues and the Incite Focus Fab Lab works specifically to innovate solutions to community problems. The program provides opportunities to youths who are transforming entire neighborhoods. But interestingly, one project that gave purpose and meaning to local kids in the United States also connected villages in South Africa to the rest of the world. A few years ago, Incite Focus built cargo bicycles and had the idea to install solar charging panels on them, turning a simple bike into a mobile charging station. Brilliant, yes, but how such an innovation is used is the real story. Fab lab founder Blair Evans had contacts in South Africa, where he knew that residents of rural villages who lived without electricity were being sold electronic devices. Through local connections, Incite Focus sold its "mobile charging stations" to micro-entrepreneurs who could afford a bicycle that didn't need gasoline. They could ride from village to village, making a few pennies for their services. With this beautiful cycle, kids in Detroit are helping industrious South Africans start small businesses that support their families and give villagers internet and cellphone connections.

Designing Solutions to Environmental Problems

Speaking of electronics, have you ever wondered where old cellphones, computers, laptops and tablets go to die? Often, countries like Togo or Ghana with relaxed environmental laws are paid by the West to dispose of machines filled with heavy metals and chemicals. WoeLab, a fab lab in Togo, recognized the problem and came up with a creative solution. Before eWaste is burned — which creates environmental and health problems for the population — WoeLab scavenges useable parts from the dumps. They have created designs for 3D printers using eWaste parts, and the finished machines are donated to schools throughout the country.

Catalysts for Inner City Development

I first met Neil Didriksen, chief operating officer of the Robert W. Deutsch Foundation, at a Digital Fabrication Summit organized by Potomac Photonics in May 2014. He had attended the event to learn more about fab labs. Didriksen and his wife, Jane Brown, run the Deutsch Foundation — the legacy of Brown's father's innovation in medical device technology — and they wanted to use digital fabrication technology to transform underserved Baltimore communities. When I visited the old warehouse in the Greenmount West neighborhood of Baltimore, I was skeptical that a thriving fab lab could exist in such an abandoned area. But the Deutsch Foundation was committed to the inner city, and it brought in stakeholders who knew exactly what would work in their community. When I returned for the grand opening and a Mini Maker Faire in fall 2016, the change in the neighborhood was palpable. Open Works Baltimore is now the anchor for education and entrepreneurship in an area that has a long history of manufacturing. It has just gotten started but has already seen programs take off. It will be an adventure to track Open Works's journey.

Another Baltimore Fab Lab, at the Community College of Baltimore County (CCBC), was the design and fabrication site for the senior capstone project of University of Maryland, Baltimore County (UMBC) mechanical engineering student Brandon Wagner. His adviser, Govind Rao, is the director of the Center for Advanced Sensor Technology at UMBC. Through work in his native India with Phoenix Medical Systems, Rao developed a partnership to help save the lives of newborn babies. Health and safety conditions in rural hospitals were poor and in many cases babies were kept warm just under the heat of a light bulb. Wagner explained to me that the base cost of American incubators is in the $20,000 range before any bells and whistles are added. To reduce costs, he needed to design an incubator that was limited to only one function: maintaining consistent temperature.

Grand opening at Open Works Fab Lab in Baltimore. Courtesy of P. Boisvert.

Professor Rao understood the need to involve the local medical community in the design rather than rely on experts half a world away. It was interesting that the midwives consulted at the hospital requested that the incubator not be too robust because of the possibility it might spread disease. Technology such as Western-style incubators is often re-used without the sanitation methods needed for newborns, whose immune systems are compromised. Brandon decided that a disposable incubator made the most sense. Simple materials and methods had to be a priority in the design, since the cost for the baby chamber parts had to stay below $20. Since cardboard is thermally efficient and can fold for shipping, it was the material of choice for the area that came in contact with the infant. Initially, Brandon recalls, they used just a box-cutter to make the enclosures, but then he decided to automate and looked for a CNC machine. Buying one was cost-prohibitive, but he discovered Fab Lab Baltimore, which gave him machine access and a place to store the project. Reuseable components such as the heater, sensors, scale, etc., ended up costing about $200 total. With the help of Fab Lab Baltimore, a disposable incubator that can reduce neonatal mortality in India and other rural areas was born out of an engineering student's ingenuity and willingness to listen to the end user.

Led by entrepreneur-in-residence Netia McCray, Fab Lab Roxbury hosts workshops that give participants a product design and development crash course. The fab lab is part of the Roxbury Innovation Center serving Boston's inner city. Embracing project-based learning's requirement to be authentic for the students, McCray starts the workshop with a visit to neighborhood grocery store, Tropical Foods, which serves as the "client" for the new products. She leads everyone through a market research exercise that identifies areas of the store that need improvement. From signage to carts, the young people review how the store could better serve customers, especially the elderly. Back at the fab lab, designs are made in CAD, then rapid-prototyped via laser cutting, 3D printing, microelectronics or micro milling. My personal favorite combined a motion sensor with enhanced controls to create a safer grocery-cart experience.

The Center of European Fab Labs

Fab Lab Barcelona, in Spain, is one of the most active fab labs in the network, handling Fab Academy administration and coordinating many functions for the Fab Foundation. It hosts a vibrant making community and offers three- to six-month internships for anyone who needs help bringing an idea to fruition. Aaron Makaruk is an entrepreneur lucky enough to have spent time at Fab Lab Barcelona refining designs for his open-source agricultural products. Having worked with Marcin Jakubowski, the founder of Open Source Ecology, Aaron had concepts to create open-source designs for urban gardens and beekeeping. He recalls, "In the three months of the internship, Fab Lab Barcelona provided administrative support and access to the machines, including CNC. But most powerful for me was being able to work alongside elite designers solving problems and optimizing digital files for the best results." Aaron is now co-founder and CEO of Aker in Denver, making and selling products along with supplying open source files. They just completed a successful Kickstarter for a beehive sensor that allows beekeepers to monitor their hives remotely, and they have more ideas for open source solutions to ecological problems.

Smart Citizen is an environmental-sensing platform product coming directly out of Fab Lab Barcelona, where design and prototyping have led to sale of about 1,000 units. Co-founders Tomas Diez and Alex Posada are steeped in the fab lab world and are also pioneers in the fab city concept launched in Barcelona. Fab cities strive to be sustainable by harnessing the means of production for local consumption. Smart Citizen is a perfect tool for anyone wanting to make a city or even a neighborhood fab or smart. Sensors that measure air composition (CO_2 and NO_2), temperature, humidity, light intensity and sound levels provide the data that support community participation, leading to citizen engagement and even co-governance.

With shared data, local citizens can interact with and even shape dialogue regarding the activities of daily life. One user in Tucson, Ariz., was looking to use Smart Citizen as a resident exchange that would bolster community building. More tools like Smart Citizen will be a strong element of the fab city project, which has been embraced from Boston to Shenzhen, China.

San Diego Lab Supports Veteran Population

With near perfect weather and deep-water ports, San Diego is home to a thriving military economy. Not surprisingly, the region boasts one of the nation's largest concentrations of military veterans and it sounds to me like one of the most appealing places to retire or leave active duty. Fab Lab San Diego reflects the military demographic, with active duty military or veterans making up 20 percent of its membership. Former Navy corpsman Alan McAfee, who worked as the fab lab's operations manager, created an entrepreneur-in-residence program to encourage veterans with product and service ideas to collaborate and support one another. It was a clever way to get volunteers, since the participants were required to donate at least five hours per week at the lab in exchange for access to the tools and space.

"There is something interesting about the intersection of the maker movement and the veteran population," said Katie Rast in a *New York Times* interview. A founder of Fab Lab San Diego, Rast added, "I think there is a call to action that really speaks to those who have served, knowing you have been the creator of something that has use in the world[24]." As often happens in the collaborative fab lab community, McAfee met the founders of Robo3D, who had novel ideas for building 3D printers, since they were college students who didn't have the money to purchase anything that was already on the market. Fab Lab San Diego provided the Robo3D team an affordable setting to test ideas and prototype their first machine. McAfee ended up joining the company as a partner and vice president of engineering, becoming an entrepreneur himself in the process.

Providing Education for Women in Rwanda

Marie Planchard, director of education and early engagement at Dassault Systemes Solidworks, which develops and markets 3D CAD design software, brings a passion for education to her job, especially for training women and girls. So it is not surprising that Planchard was instrumental in bringing Fab Lab Rwanda to Telecom House in Kigali, Rwanda. A joint effort of Solidworks, the ICT Chamber, the Rwanda Development Board, the Japan International Cooperation Agency, the Rwanda Ministry of Education and Gasabo3D, the relatively new fab lab emphasizes education and entrepreneurship opportunities. Rwanda's population is still recovering from the genocide in its last Civil War, and President Paul Kagame's dream is to move the country from a subsistence economy to a thriving system that can support the many young people orphaned in the war. Women have suffered particularly hard and are often forced to sacrifice education to support their families. Consequently, Fab Lab Rwanda actively engages women as managers to run programs and to teach skills. Solidworks has a history of supporting women's education in Rwanda, having funded three-year scholarships for girls to attend the Nyanza Technical School. Many of the girls have been able to further their education, and at least one, Monique Uwambajimana, has become an entrepreneur. With help from Solidworks's marketing department, she founded a business that helped her fellow Rwandans: NURU Energy, a socially driven enterprise, which provides rechargeable LED lights as an environmentally sound, inexpensive and safe alternative to the kerosene lamps used in Rwandan homes. Two Solidworks employees personally sent Monique the funds for her start-up costs. She now sells the lights at a low cost to villages and recharges them with a pedal-powered device for a low fee, allowing her to literally run her business and help her community at the same time.

Entrepreneurship in America's Heartland

Fab labs have helped other entrepreneurs, too. Jim Correll was most likely selected by Independence Community College (ICC) in Independence, Kan., to lead a new entrepreneurship program because of his strong start-up background and the 15 years he spent working in manufacturing. When the Fab Lab ICC was added to the program, Correll was the logical choice to become director of the hybrid student- and membership-based community organization. At about that time he founded the National Association for Community College Entrepreneurship, and his business development ideas were strengthened. Correll told me he wants to "develop a stable of entrepreneurs so that they can fulfill the work that naturally comes to the fab lab. Then ideas might develop and a new business is born." One example is a woman who learned laser engraving in the fab lab and now has a business coding and marking customized products. One of her biggest customers is Cobalt Boats, which makes luxury sport boats in Kansas. Correll said that he basically "set up the environment as a catalyst for things to happen. No one in Fab Lab ICC cares about age or gender. It's all about sharing ideas, and then building ideas off each other." Echoing Dr. Gershenfeld's basic premise about the role of digital fabrication, Correll said that the fab lab's mission is to improve the self-efficacy of the participants. "I've found there's a lot of similarity between the maker and entrepreneurial mindsets. The fab lab gives everyone a safe place to fail and learn from their mistakes." Believing in one's own ability to achieve is important for members who are autistic or learning challenged, as well as for entrepreneurs. Correll explained, "Building a company is a lonely job sometimes, and founders need a support system to give them the confidence to go forward." In Fab Lab ICC, entrepreneurs not only have access to tools for prototyping their product ideas, but they also have tools for economically creating marketing communications such as banners, trade show signage, business cards and promotional materials. Along with this Jim has developed an entrepreneurial mindset class, so he is helping members both on the technical side and on what many call the "soft skills" side as well.

A Floating Fab Lab Covers the Amazon

Rural communities sometimes face unusual challenges in creating fab labs. Some rural communities are only accessible by water. This is true along the mighty Amazon River, whose basin covers 40 percent of South America's land mass. FABLAT, a network of fab labs in South America, has responded to the needs of communities along the Amazon and to increasing contamination from industry, especially oil and gas spills, by creating the floating fab lab. Designed to get to the most remote regions of the Amazon, a floating fab lab can help local groups monitor water safety, ideate sustainable farming methods and educate the next generation in the use of new tools. One of the most creative projects involves a biosensor bracelet that children can wear to test for heavy metal levels in the water.

Building Humanitarian Aid on Site

The Global Humanitarian Lab, or GHL, embodies problem-solving of the broadest and deepest scope to address some of the world's most challenging issues. A joint effort of leading international relief organizations, governments, nonprofits and the private sector, the organization is administered as a partnership within the United Nations Office for Project Services, and its governing board is composed of representatives from each of the founding groups. Peter Maurer, president of the International Committee of the Red Cross (ICRC), is the board chairperson. Co-founder David Ott is also based at the ICRC and is the liaison to the Fab Lab Network. GHL's mission is to accelerate humanitarian innovation in response to ever-growing needs from disasters, wars and population displacement. The magnitude of the problem makes collaborative innovation imperative; otherwise, efforts might be fragmented and duplicated, leading to large-scale inefficiencies and waste.

Getting donated aid and supplies de-
livered to the people who need them
is a major problem in humanitarian
work. Delivery is often impossible to
remote areas that may also be dangerous, especially in the case of war.
Goods often end up on the black market, which does not help the intended

David Ott (left), co-founder of Global
Humanitarian Lab, working with designers
at DigiFabCon. Courtesy of P. Boisvert.

constituency. Think instead of making in-demand items — medical supplies such as splints and braces, signage, temporary shelters — right on
the spot where they are needed. A portable fab lab that has cutting, drilling, 3D printing and other capabilities can answer humanitarian needs
and also foster innovation within the affected communities.

MIT Fab Lab Supports Student Innovators

Products have also come out of the fab lab at MIT's Center for Bits
and Atoms, or CBA. This lab is not open to the public but is a university
research lab where many students are completing master's and Ph.D.
degrees with Professor Gershenfeld. The level of innovation in making
technology available to society makes it interesting. Graduate students
Maxim Lobovsky, Natan Linder and David Cranor met as students at
the CBA while taking Gershenfeld's "How to Make (almost) Anything"
class. They were interested in stereolithography, or SLA, the first type
of 3D printing. Partly because this type of additive manufacturing is
based on a sophisticated laser process, the machines are expensive and
large. The MIT students thought they could miniaturize the process,
producing an SLA printer with a tabletop footprint and a reasonable
cost. Deciding to fund development through the new Kickstarter platform, the Form1 was born with a record-shattering $3 million in crowd
funding and with a large percentage of equipment pre-sales coming
from the maker community. Formlabs is now extending the product
line with 3D printers for specific market segments such as dental and

jewelry products and an affordable selective laser-sintering 3D printer. Listening to the needs of manufacturers, Formlabs is developing the Form Cell system, which integrates everything needed for successful printing in one package. From an automated dashboard to multiple Form2 SLA machines, print failure detection, and a post-processing station, the Form Cell is the complete product for 3D printing in a production setting.

New Collar Job Training at Fab Labs

FabForce is a digital fabrication training certificate set up by Jim Correll at Independence Community College's Fab Lab. Correll said that the Fab Force Certificate combines elements of mechatronics with other skills from the entrepreneurial mindset, creative design and communication course work. It is the equivalent of about 15 credit hours and can either stand alone or enhance any other field of study. Correll has worked hard to integrate non-technical skills with welding, machining, 3D printing, CAD design, robotics and electronics. Starting with his work on the entrepreneurial mindset, he also includes creative thinking, communication, conflict resolution and character. That last trait is perhaps more mentioned than anything else by employers today, and it covers showing up to work on time, contributing fully and being a responsible member of the staff.

The entrepreneurial mindset portion of the Fab Force program works because it is reinforced in the fab lab's hands-on activities. Learning about being an entrepreneur is one thing, but doing it is quite another, and those of us who have done it have battle scars to show. Fab Lab ICC not only helps inventors rapidly prototype new products, but tools are available to print business cards, marketing communications materials, and promotional signs and banners. Correll is an active participant in the Ice House Entrepreneurship Program from the Entrepreneurial Learning Initiative (ELI), which was developed from the hard-learned lessons of a real-life entrepreneur. The methodology

Tim Voegeli, entrepreneur in Independence (Mo.) Community College Fab Lab. Courtesy of
ICC Fab Lab.

sounds to me a lot like the scientific method we employed at Potomac
Photonics. Correll described the Ice House way as starting small and
then seeing if an idea works. Instead of million-dollar angel or venture
capital investments and quick market gains, this is an incremental process that fits well with many types of products.

Correll used the Ice House way of thinking when a Wichita resident came to Fab Lab ICC's for help with rapid prototyping capabilities. Correll calls it his disruption story. First of all, he's quite proud
that someone from a city many times the size of Independence came
to his small town for business help. The big-city inventor had an idea
to produce a plastic clip that would help bicyclists change tires more
easily. Correll remembered that in five weeks, they printed out seven
different design changes, finally hitting on a winning product. That's
an example of true iterative design in action. Since the fab lab has the
capability to manufacture small production runs, the new entrepreneur
manufactured 50 sets of the clips to pass out to potential customers and

dealers to test the market potential. The iterative design process that is inherent to digital fabrication ensured that the final product was the best design the company could take to market. But it was the Fab Lab ICC's complete process that closed the loop from rapid prototyping to market research to promotion.

Fab Labs go to College

In 2016, Century College, a community college in White Bear Lake, Minn., saw its state-of-the-art, $1.1 million Engineering and Fab Lab/ Innovation Center as an ideal place to launch an associate's degree in additive and digital manufacturing in applied science. In addition to the tools required in every fab lab, the facility has added advanced capabilities aimed at training manufacturing operators and technicians, including automated manufacturing cells, industrial process control systems and advanced diagnostic equipment. Requiring 60 credits for graduation, the degree is comprehensive, and although it can be completed at a full or part time pace, the commitment is substantial. "The additive and digital manufacturing program was developed to train our students to solve technical problems in today's manufacturing environments," said faculty member Scott Simenson, who is also director of the fab lab. The curriculum is a mix of technical and "soft" skills. For example, the summer internship in designing and building in the fab lab also covers resume writing, creating a LinkedIn profile and oral presentations.

Another comprehensive program with a specific subject focus is an associate of applied science degree in laser and optics technology offered at Indian Hills Community College in Ottumwa, Iowa. Laser industry colleagues introduced me to Greg Kepner, chair of Indian Hills's Advanced Manufacturing Technology Department in early 2017. As we talked in the Laser Institute of America booth at the Photonics West Expo, it was like being with a rock star. A steady stream of executives from optics and laser companies stopped to share compliments about the well-trained students who were working for them from the Indian Hills program. The big request was for more students to fill the many job openings in the industry. Kepner said that the key to success for training operators and technicians is hands-on experience in the lab. During the 21-month degree course, students spend at least 40 percent of their time working directly with lasers and optical systems. Having spent my career working with light, I can attest that photonics requires unique technical knowledge, and although non-specialists at Potomac Photonics were able to succeed, it would have saved us quite a lot of on-the-job training to start with an Indian Hills graduate.

Aerospace Training Looking up in Florida

The father and daughter engineers who founded and guide the Space Coast Fab Lab bring a strong relationship with the aerospace industry to training programs at three locations on Florida's East Coast near Cape Canaveral. Being in the midst of companies that often need very specific tool skills, Space Coast Fab Lab has developed machine-specific training for which jobs are available right in the neighborhood.

Dave and Tabitha Beavers are a dynamic duo. With a degree in electrical engineering, Tabitha Beavers works in innovation and transformation program management at the Northrop Grumman Corp. in Melourne. Her father seems to be "retired" from the industry that serves NASA locally, but that's a relative term. Dave Beavers knows how to get equipment donations better than anyone I know. When I visited the most recent addition to their family of fab labs, he had what seemed like a warehouse of technology. "I'll take anything," he said. "If I can't use it, I can usually find a buyer, and then get the cash we need to purchase the specific tool I'm looking for." Pick-and-place electronics machines that cost hundreds of thousands of dollars, for example, have been donated to facilitate a certificate program to train operators. Of course, Dave Beavers makes it all look much easier than we know it is in reality but his gift for wheeling and dealing technology tools translates to solid training for people on Florida's Space Coast that could lead to work for companies that help NASA explore the outer reaches of the universe.

Joining Forces with Fab Lab

In our early history, Potomac Photonics had ties to Washington, D.C., due to our early R&D funding projects with the federal government. But by the time Mike Adelstein took over the helm, the situation had changed. He recognized that a new chapter in the company would be tied to the vibrant community developing around the University of Maryland, Baltimore County, of which he was an alumnus. Adelstein moved the company to UMBC South, a tech campus that offered amenities to the growing company. The new facility was located about a mile from the Community College of Baltimore County (CCBC) where Fab Lab Baltimore is located. The two groups were a perfect match. Like many fab labs in the international Fab Lab Network, FLB found itself trying to create a sustainable business model and to grow the company. Potomac Photonics needed operators and technicians. Space and equipment may be easy to come by, but operating funds are hard to procure for fab labs, and talent with experience in digital fabrication is in short supply for manufacturers.

Fab lab founder Ken Burch realized he had to involve the local manufacturing community in a sustainability dialog to find viable solutions for each. So, he invited Adelstein to be part of a new FLB advisory board. "After seeing FLB's people resources, I realized working together was a good fit," said Adelstein. "We had the full complement of fab lab tools, including 3D printing, laser marking and CNC machining, but we didn't have the staff to work on the larger spatial-scale jobs that come to us organically through our digital fabrication reputation. Even for our micro-fabrication jobs we need packaging and identification, which is perfect for the fab lab skill set." Ken Burch added, "We needed to be able to demonstrate to CCBC that FLB could sustain itself so the partnership with Potomac Photonics was obvious. What I didn't expect was that the collaboration with Potomac Photonics would give our people new skills and insight that they would bring back to FLB and apply to other industrial settings."

Internships are key to Potomac Photonics' hiring practices for digital fabrication staff. Courtesy of Potomac Photonics Inc.

Producing anything when on-time delivery with high quality is essential to customer satisfaction develops an entirely new level of skills that is much different from a classroom theoretical exercise.

Mike Adelstein said that, "The interns they hired were quick studies, but most importantly, demonstrated solid skills under production pressure. We were able move up some of them quickly to more sophisticated work for the company such as laser micromachining." While Potomac Photonics doesn't stray often from its focus on micro-manufacturing, occasionally there is a strategic reason to take a macro-scale job. Sometimes these projects are to enhance community connections, such as when the city of Annapolis, Md., needed to laser mark sailboat-shaped bike racks with designs created by a former intern.

Adelstein pointed out that the paid interns start their first day on the job with basic digital fabrication skills such as reading CAD files, setting up machines for jobs and solving problems. The students can work independently when they start, which is valuable in a production setting, and he added they have an amazing work ethic. The CCBC program is part of a two-year associate of applied science degree in design, fabrication and advanced manufacturing, with a core curriculum of four courses: digital fabrication fundamentals; advanced digital fabrication; integrated fabrication and design/build technology; and next generation-manufacturing strategies. The courses cover topics that include CAD design, operating basic digital fabrication tools such as laser cutters, 3D printers, and CNC machines, building a functional prototype, and selecting the right tool for a specific job, dimensional stability, material properties and part tolerances.

In an ingenious move to channel operating funds to the fab lab, Adelstein, who also happens to be a certified public accountant, hires students through the fab lab rather than as direct employees. In that way he can add overhead and general and administrative expenses to the total price, giving FLB a little bit of revenue beyond the student fee to help pay for the program. Fab lab founder Ken Burch found that beyond providing additional revenue, the intern program builds workers who are now readily employable with the extra skills — such as quality control — that they learned at Potomac Photonics. Of course, Potomac Photonics is one of the first to snap up FLB interns and bring them in as full-time staff. Burch finds that since the interns are paid for their time and expertise, they are also happier and have a better attitude. The students achieve self-efficacy in the win-win public-private partnership.

CHAPTER TWELVE
Where the Entrepreneur and Maker Meet

I was raised in an entrepreneurial household. My dad was an entrepreneur in the textile dyestuff business who taught me that I could do anything. As a kid, I started reading *The Wall Street Journal*, which was a staple in our house, to find topics to discuss with my dad while doing the dishes or watching the Red Sox, since he was an introvert who who had to be drawn into conversation. By the time I went to business school I had covered nearly everything about running a business with my father, who had done it all. That said, I have always felt my greatest strengths are analytical thinking and discipline, which, I suspect, were developed studying to be a concert pianist. Before I helped Potomac Photonics build lasers or 3D-printed jewelry in the fab lab, I made music, but I was still using my hands. And therein lies the connection.

To me, entrepreneurship and making share a similar mindset with many overlapping traits. First and foremost, both entrepreneurs and fabricators make things happen. An employee once told me, "Lots of people have great ideas, but you make yours happen." Makers jump in and run a CNC machine and don't feel like they need to complete a Ph.D. before using it. Going out with friends is far less interesting to me than bringing a creation to life, whether it's a prototype or an ad campaign. Start-up founders may be called workaholics, but most of my colleagues in this crazy space genuinely love the creating process. Just as a maker may stay in the shop all weekend to finish a project, entrepreneurs put in the time and energy required to finish a job. In both mindsets, trying something that might fail is a viable way to get started, and if it doesn't work, we learn from the experience and either progress or go to something else.

Entrepreneurship and making both require focus. I see so many people who can't stay on a path. A colleague once introduced me to an inventor who needed advice on getting funding for 60 products. A big company will struggle with introducing even two or three new products, so there is no hope for a start-up successfully designing and marketing 60. In order to design and build anything, a maker must focus on the task at hand, especially, of course, where potentially dangerous tools are involved. If one is going to make something happen it's also imperative to know what's important in the process. It's so easy to get sidetracked into interesting distractions that don't move you forward. You'll hear business owners say the hardest word to say is "No." It is especially hard to say no to new opportunities that are not part of the overall company strategy or that do not provide profitable revenue.

Entrepreneurs and makers learn fast that it is best to recognize our skills and either find professional help or training in areas where we do not excel. One of Dr. Christensen's strongest traits as an entrepreneur was seeking the marketing expertise that he didn't have, and trusting my skills. Empowering the people with whom we work is another essential maker and entrepreneurial skill, and that really starts with respect. If we respect our colleagues and employees, we trust that they can be part of the problem-solving process and lead us to innovation that we never dreamed was possible.

Fab Lab Hub is a marriage of those entrepreneurial and maker mindsets. After the sale of Potomac Photonics, I was consulting and living in semi-retirement when the requests started coming in for me to help starting maker spaces. I guess the rationale was that I had used all the digital fabrication tools so I must know something about it. I was familiar with Neil Gershenfeld's work as Potomac Photonics had built laser micro-machining workstations for other departments at MIT. And so I set out to learn more about the current state of fab labs, thereby meeting Sherry Lassiter, director of the Fab Foundation. My conclusion was that if a maker space had no constraints to do otherwise, becoming a part of the Fab Lab Network was a wise decision. In helping to start about six fab labs in New England, I was engaged by the Fab Foundation to consult on marketing communications and fundraising. As I worked more with the international network, my analytical mind started to think about the needs of the community. All start-ups should be an answer to a customer need, and so to me this was just natural entrepreneurial behavior. As often happens in life, the needs of a related group, manufacturers who seek skilled workers, intersected, and I had that "ah ha!" moment.

Fab Lab Hub facilitates new clollar job training programs to meet the manufacturing industry's need for operators and technicians through alternative project-based learning and entrepreneurial thinking programs in fab labs and maker spaces that are appealing to young people. We operate model labs in New Mexico to prove new concepts and share knowledge, methodologies, and marketing support via an online Digital Fabrication Alliance.

In our own fab lab, we offer training that earns digital badges, which are validated certifications of accomplishment. I had seen the success of

Design Swarms Workshop organized by Fab Lab Hub. Courtesy of P. Boisvert.

the Potomac Photonics paid internship program with Fab Lab Baltimore and knew this kind of real-world experience was essential to our success. However, depending on and coordinating with industry is a challenge, and while we do have partnerships with local companies, Fab Lab Hub actually includes a commercial job shop. In this way, we can have on-site training and generate funds to pay for interns, equipment maintenance and operating supplies. Several of our vendors have verified that equipment in high schools is generating sufficient revenue to support training programs. Having operated the Potomac Photonics job shop, I understand the market, which is national in size. Anywhere that FedEx or UPS ship holds potential customers, which is a boon to a rural area. Today, people shop online and care most about quality, delivery and price. Rapid prototyping, jewelry molds for casting, signs, wearables, reward engraving, CAD file generation and other small products can be quickly and easily produced in the job shop. The pay scale for interns is well above the minimum wage, and talented students have the inside track for full-time jobs. From my own experience in taking a start-up to a successful exit, I also teach "How to Make a Business in a Fab Lab," a course that takes the student from concept to prototype and marketing plan. In the future we expect our apprenticeship program to be approved by the U. S. Dept. of Labor, expanding the internships from a semester to two years. We have also developed on-line courses. Much like the more comprehensive Fab Academy taught by Neil Gershenfeld, 3D printer service technician training for veterans incorporates video conferencing class work with homework in a local fab lab or maker space.

CHAPTER THIRTEEN
Alternative
Training Programs

I find most political speeches boring, but all that changed when, in a State of the Union address, President Barack Obama mentioned the Additive Manufacturing Institute that his administration had created in Youngstown, Ohio as part of its Manufacturing USA program. For someone working in advanced manufacturing, to hear a new technology called out on national TV was pretty exciting. Established in 2012, America Makes, as the Youngstown facility is named, is the flagship Institute for the Manufacturing USA initiative. It is a public-private partnership that innovates and accelerates additive manufacturing with the goal of increasing our nation's global manufacturing competitiveness. The organization convenes the leading minds in 3D printing to map out and lead the future of additive R&D, coordinates information to facilitate technical and training programs and catalyzes the industry through collaborative projects that deliver high value and impact. In the last few years I've heard companies from HP to Autodesk and start-ups to academic researchers say this topic is so big and daunting that no one can tackle it alone. Buying an additive manufacturing machine is one thing, but the more important issues are training staff, developing industry standards, complying with government regulations and advancing the technology so that it is accepted on the factory floor.

America Makes provides a platform for the kind of collaboration needed to ensure the industrywide success of a technology that changes the playing field for manufacturing.

Education and training are central to new technology adoption. As I heard time and again during my research, "That new 3D printer looks great, but who in my company is going to operate it?" America

Makes instituted the Academi program to answer that question. Operators and technicians trained in the Academi courses will learn how to get a 3D printer up and running, troubleshoot any issues and solve problems as they arise in real-world manufacturing situations. The fundamental course is a one-to-two-week intensive modular foundational curriculum that can be customized to the students' needs. It is held at the America Makes innovation factory in Youngstown, which houses just about every type and brand of 3D printer manufactured today. Academi integrates lectures and labs with project-based learning to give students a comprehensive educational experience. In collaboration with the Air Force, the Academi also offers a capstone module around an end user's specific needs. Because America Makes is not a commercial manufacturing company, it can envision the bigger picture of just how additive manufacturing fits with other manufacturing technologies. As a result, Academi students are not learning just about 3D printing but also how additive manufacturing assimilates into an integrated set of tools to facilitate adoption by industries. Academi is a systems approach to learning that America Makes intends to yield the strongest result for next-generation factory workers.

Leading industry collaboration, America Makes has partnered with member organizations to advance several important areas. Together with SME, the Society of Manufacturing Engineers, it is working on two certifications: additive manufacturing fundamentals and additive manufacturing technician. These consist of modules that can be taken individually, then stacked to master the principles and processes needed to earn the certificate. Both certifications utilized the AM Body of Knowledge that industry groups, the Milwaukee School of Engineering and over 500 industry professionals working in the field created. Certifications are becoming more important in education as people reject multiyear associate and undergraduate degrees in favor of flexible platforms for specific new collar jobs. The addition of AM makes sense as the society provides several other manufacturing certifications in its Tooling-U education program. America Makes is also collaborating with the American National Standards Institute (ANSI) to set standards for AM. Together they formed the America Makes and ANSI Additive Manufacturing Standardization Collaborative (AMSC) to facilitate the large-scale effort that signals a level of maturation in the industry.

One of America Makes's more inspiring collaborations is with 3D Veterans. The brainchild of David Schnepp, a former 3D Systems business development manager, and Michael Moncada, an Army Medical Corps veteran, the start-up offers workforce training and job placement in 3D printing at no charge to veterans. Financial support comes from America Makes and the U.S. Department of Veterans Affairs Center for Innovation. As I found in our research, 3D printing is growing, and operators and technicians to run the machines need training. Re-entering civilian life is a challenge for veterans, many of whom have been injured in war. Updating skills for new collar job opportunities can jump-start a career or give someone with an idea a platform for starting a business. The 3D Veterans model is rooted in project-based learning that is authentic for the participants. Obviously, designing and 3D printing assistive devices for injured servicemen and women is one project category that hits close to home.

Retired U.S. Army Major Joshua Munch, who spent 17 years in the service, had many opportunities to observe injured soldiers. One simple task that struck him was the inability for anyone with hand or finger injuries or missing limbs to drink from a straw. To help the disabled do this, Major Munch designed and prototyped a cup clip for holding a straw in place. With advice from his far-hipper children, the design evolved to include animals and other features, moving the device from the realm of purely functional to cool. Who wouldn't use a straw holder that was also a fashion statement? Other products designed and 3D-printed in the class included a lightweight attachment at the ankle providing more comfortable leg prosthetics and a tool case for diabetics developed by former Army Military Intelligence Officer Shawn

Tillman. Future improvements could include storing insulin in the new case at stable temperatures. Fab Lab Hub is proud to be an America Makes member and is looking forward to working together to develop additional advanced new collar job training.

In preparation for writing this book, I visited several training facilities. I was totally awed by the additive manufacturing and rapid prototyping centers at the University of Louisville. An engineer at heart, I was able to "geek out" with Ed Tackett, director of educational programs in additive manufacturing, and Tim Gornet, manager of the Rapid Prototyping Center. First of all, the combined labs have every kind of additive manufacturing tool one could find today. Tackett boasts of several high-end, metal 3D printers that represent millions of dollars in machinery. Gornet has everything from a Formlabs Form2 up to a selective laser-melting 3D printer from EOS. Each lab has a slightly different focus but they are jointly increasing the much-needed pool of users in the field.

The RPC works with U of L graduate students and industry users on research and development, as well as training. Since 1993, RPC's emphasis has been on rapid prototyping in the additive manufacturing space, so Gornet is a perfect fit. He is a 3D-printing pioneer, having used the technology at GE back in the late 1980s, just a few years after it was invented. The key to his work with graduate students involves project-based learning and simulation studies. Tackett's work is dedicated to intensive training for industry and technical professionals. For the initial courses, the University of Louisville partnered on advanced AM metals training, which is a tremendous industry need. As the price of entry-level metal printers drops and more companies adopt additive manufacturing, there is an even wider gap in metal 3D-printing skills. For plastic and other materials, kids may play with small FDM machines and colleges may have SLS or SLA printers. But metal printers are harder to come by, meaning fewer people have exposure to their idiosyncrasies. Metal 3D printing is the most challenging of the additive variations and has greater safety risks, including flammable metal powders that can ignite when heated by the thermal laser process. The intensive one-week, hands-on class covers every aspect of metal 3D printing, which is easy for Tackett, since he worked as the director of The RapidTech Center at the Henry Samueli School of Engineering at the University of California, Irvine, for 18 years. "The goal of the class," he told me, "is understanding we have to control the process. We go through check-off sheets and establish internal standard operating procedures. Metal AM operators have to understand the process end-to-end, from particle size analysis of the powders to post-processing and how to deal with handling residual waste. We want to up-scale a machinist so that he or she becomes a valuable team member. Sure, we can teach someone to print just about any file they're handed, but the main question is, "Is it functional?" so the machinist can supply feedback to the designer to optimize the print. When we're working with million-dollar 3D printers, it's expensive if parts don't work."

Tackett rates old-school machinists as some of the best students, because they're used to looking at the mechanical properties of parts and how they function. The transition to a new manufacturing method doesn't change the underlying principles for them. A standard operating procedure is even more critical when working with machines where there is little company history or know-how, and no old industry veterans to tap for help. Course attendees are given guidelines and an SOP, so they have a jump-start on the job and understand the underlying issues with the machines, enabling them to run jobs more efficiently. Tackett and Gornet are pragmatic, an essential trait when training people for industrial applications, especially in a field known for its cool factor.

For full disclosure, I must say that I have a long history using Autodesk products. Potomac Photonics first designed our lasers and laser micromachining workstations in AutoCAD. Of course, in the late 1990s, that's really all that was available to us. We had to switch the company to PCs from Macs to meet the software's requirements (I bought a Mac laptop the moment we sold the company!), but AutoCAD is still used at Potomac Photonics all these decades later, because it is a solid tool for our contract manufacturing work. As my own fabrication has moved more to 3D printing and become more collaborative, I've discovered the versatility of new Autodesk programs in my lab. What has impressed me the most in the evolution of Autodesk software is the company's commitment to education and advancing the industry above their own narrow interests.

In looking for a workshop at DigiFabCon, Fab Lab Hub's annual meeting in the U.S., I was fortunate enough to be introduced to Sunand Bhattacharya. This soft-spoken gentleman who exudes old world gentility is the Global Education Strategist for the Autodesk Education Experience Group of more than 100 people that serves as a catalyst for change in the industry through education. We immediately hit it off since we spoke the same education and innovation language. Bhattacharya's philosophy is that if people are given the tools to design anytime, anyplace, they can create amazing things. In this view, it is not about the individual tool or product; it's about what we do with tools. This is startlingly evident in the recent opening of the Autodesk BUILD Space in Boston's revived Seaport district. Occupying an old waterfront warehouse, the BUILD Space is a collaborative place where builders can design and fabricate ideas focused on the construction industry. What was most interesting to me was that entrepreneurs in residence and interns weren't required to be married to Autodesk software. On a tour last year, I learned that innovators could use any software they liked as long as they were advancing the state of the art. And, of course, that's when the magic happens. Bhattacharya explained that as technology becomes more accessible, people become change agents. His group creates new ways for people to think and develop a design mindset. It's not all just about engineers, but rather about better work flow for anyone with an idea. Bhattacharya then introduced me to Fusion 360. Because Fusion exists in the cloud, groups in Mumbai and Arizona State University working on the same project can collaborate in real time.

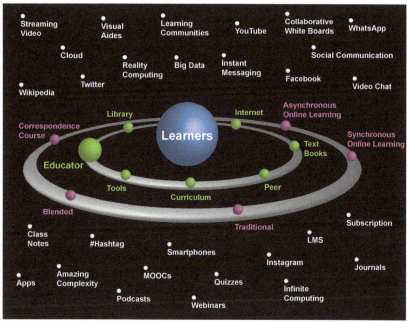

The learning universe of today's students. Image by Devon Unwin. Concept used with permission from Sunand Bhattacharya.

This increases the speed and quality of iterative design. Also, groups can work offline and connect later, and, most appealingly, innovators can design in a non-geometric space, quickly defining organic shapes to make ideation quicker.

Bhattacharya told me that academia needs to prepare for the next generation of learners who have been raised on a digital diet and are hungry to innovate and make products. With the internet, stories of their peers creatively solving personal and community problems are rampant, and young people want to participate in this culture. He loves to share the story of a student named Jakob, whom he met at NuVu Studios in Cambridge, Mass. NuVu is a new kind of school, a full-time "innovation school" for middle- and high-school students that uses the architectural studio model of hands-on, project-based learning. Autodesk has a Fusion 360 collaboration with the teachers and students who are designing and prototyping products. A few, like Jakob, turn their ideas into businesses. Bhattacharya described Jakob as "a 14-year-old maker, engineer and budding entrepreneur. He created GyRings, a fidget widget that allows someone with ADHD to focus on the task at hand. Using Fusion software, he physically made his idea but didn't stop there. Jakob continued designing, incorporating comments from people who played with them until finally he decided it was ready to launch." To underscore his support of the GyRings, Bhattacharya's group purchases them as giveaways for events.

CHAPTER FOURTEEN
Shaping the Future Together

Now that advanced manufacturing technologies are ubiquitous, the means of production are rapidly changing. Consumers prize customization and individual utility over a name brand and are willing to pay more in time and money to be part of a new cultural norm.

According to Bhattacharya, "The very nature of things themselves is changing. By 2020, it's predicted that there will be 50 billion web-connected devices. Agility, mobility, connection—that's what today's technology is about: cloud computing, mobile technology, social connection and collaboration. These are the trends that will dominate the years to come."

Autodesk today is not the same company that we bought AutoCAD from decades ago. It is embracing change not only with new software but also by interacting with customers and young potential customers to shape the future. As Bhattacharya said, "Historically, the workforce is dependent upon academia for graduates who can perform and contribute to their employers. But today the technically literate next generation of young people is being raised on our "apps" and other similar technologies. They are already ahead of the curve of higher ed. If we are not careful, these young people will find higher education disappointing, and so Autodesk's Future of Learning program is enabling K-12 and higher education to develop an innovative and productive society. The future is what we make it. In my opinion it is very bright."

Design Swarms Take a Team Approach

Bhattacharya graciously hosted a workshop at DigiFabCon that used design thinking to solve a relevant problem in the Fab Lab Network. He brought in Surya Vanka, former head of user experience for Microsoft who had recently founded Design Swarms, a method of team design, and my view of design thinking has not been the same since. As Vanka explains it, "Design Swarming is a new technique that combines the power of design thinking and the nimbleness of hacking into an agile problem-solving technique that produces disruptive breakthroughs. Design Swarms are small teams that move quickly through the envisioning, experimenting and validating cycle to arrive at a Validated Design Concept in a single morning or an afternoon."

Vanka and Bhattacharya spent a lot of time with us before the DigiFabCon, preparing for the Design Swarms, and I only understood the rationale once I had experienced the process. First, it is important that the group works on an authentic (that word, again!) problem. Since we had decided to hold the design-thinking workshop on short notice, we were grasping at universal problems such as maintaining a safe water supply. But none of our ideas seemed to click. We started over, reviewing the DigiFabCon content, and one speaker stood out for us: David Ott from the Humanitarian Lab. Surely the lab had pressing needs, operating in war zones, disaster areas and refugee camps. In talking with

Surya Vanka (far right) leading a Design Swarms session at DigiFabCon. Courtesy of S. Boisvert.

Ott, a not-so-sexy but essential need emerged. When he took a fab lab to an area under stress, regular delivery by FedEx, UPS or even local trucks was not an option. Ott needed to be able to package and move the fab lab tools quickly and easily to the location where fabrication was needed. Bingo, we had our challenge. Second, Vanka wanted to create the teams in advance of the workshop so that participant skills could be organized to best advantage. We ended up with four teams of five to seven people from varying backgrounds.

It turned out Design Swarms is a more highly structured process than I expected. Vanka explained it. "Each event is designed to harness the unique strengths of individuals and the collective genius of the team. It feels like fun, but I closely facilitate the progress of the teams to bring out their best ideas."

Vanka was expert at moving the teams along while giving them time to process information and transform it to viable ideas." Being trained in marketing to listen to the customer, I was most impressed that Vanka had each group create a specific person whose needs the group was trying to meet. Sticky notes have always made me a bit crazy, but as Vanka used them to share and collaborate, I started to see the brightly colored squares repurposed to represent something that could be bartered or traded. The ideas were put into design mode by Autodesk staff who were readily fluent in Fusion 360, and the graphics were beautiful.

It was a tough decision for the judges, as really everyone won, although one design from the Team Mabrimana stood out. Many of the teams had designed crates and boxes that were dual use, as one might expect would be helpful, given the situation where the fab labs were being deployed. One group's crates had built-in legs that turned the packaging into tables. Another group laser engraved the set-up instructions on the crate itself. But Team Mabrimana also saw the packaging as a way to create a safe space for women in the distressed environment to gather and feel safe. Everyone won cool swag from Autodesk, including Jakob's GyRings, but more important, came away with a new methodology for design thinking and lots of new colleagues.

Safety Certification Can Lead to Jobs

Potomac Photonics has been actively involved with the Laser Institute of America for many years, since the technical society is the Secretariat of the ANSI Laser Safety Standards, which guided our work. I served on the board of directors for many years and in 1995 was president of the board, so laser safety is instilled in me. In those early days, laser safety training materials were, of course, on paper, and all training was done on site. Today, LIA has a comprehensive program of digital training, as well as digital versions of the safety standards, guides and books. Even optical measurement practice can be learned using PDF or CD versions. As laser applications expand to surgery, education and other less technical fields, LIA has developed training and materials that are geared to the end user's industry background. The rapid growth in the number of fab labs and maker spaces has also increased the demand for laser safety in schools, community centers and youth centers. Adding laser safety officer training to an operator or technician's resume is yet one more credential in a competitive job market.

Virtual Reality's Growing Role

You would expect a 120-year-old, multibillion-dollar manufacturing equipment company to have gained expertise in training, and Lincoln Electric is now bringing 21st-century education aids into the mix. In 2009, the laser welding company responded to the decline of skilled welders in the industry by introducing a virtual reality-based machine for educating modern students. I experienced the VR welding simulator firsthand at the extensive Lincoln Campus in Cleveland. The machine provided cues such as speed, angle and aim that helped direct my progress in the simulation. I had no idea how difficult welding was but soon got used to the virtual experience, which included welding sounds and could respond to the "instructor's" real-time guidance. At the end of a session, the student is scored to measure progress, and the session can be recorded for later review. The VR simulator could be used by trade schools and in-house programs but also for recruiting, interviews and testing. Student practice doesn't waste materials, although I didn't like just getting a number score as much as holding a part in my hand. But it definitely would be a great way to practice welding skills. The VR machine is supported by a comprehensive online curriculum, student manuals, lesson plans and training classes at the Cleveland education center.

There are not very many other VR equipment simulation tools that I could find for training in manufacturing. Autodesk has worked on VR as part of the design process, and Ford has a sophisticated design-testing VR system for new vehicles. VR is used heavily in medical training — since it's difficult to practice on live patients — and in the construction industry. Part of the issue in manufacturing may be the need for substantial content for the simulator. Like manufacturers who are giving away 3D printers, unless there are accompanying applications and lessons, the simulators will not be used. The Lincoln program is quite comprehensive, so if someone has any interest in welding this is one training to investigate. Computer simulation without the VR component is available for a variety of skills, including CNC machining, robotics operation and process control, but it lacks the immersive learning experience that VR provides. For 3D printing, Solidworks includes a software add-on that simulates FDM for the student. Perhaps making training more like being in a video game with VR would attract more young people to manufacturing jobs such as welding and machining.

Production is the End Game

Since the 1930s, the Society of Manufacturing Engineers, now known only by its acronym, SME, has fostered training and education for anyone interested in skills required for manufacturing jobs. As one of the largest membership technical societies in the world dedicated to manufacturing, SME has the staff and resources to develop a wide range of workforce training programs. From online self-paced and instructor-led courses to programs designed for a manufacturer's on-site training needs and everything in between, SME is at the forefront of training for skills such as CNC machining, additive manufacturing and Lean principles. Students gain certification after completing a testing process. Collaborations with high schools, community colleges and universities are available.

"Manufacturing is changing at an accelerating pace. With the new technologies we're seeing today, the industry and our workforce are presented with new challenges; yet there are even greater opportunities to realize," said Jeff Krause, executive director and CEO, SME. "Companies that want to stay ahead of the game must invest in the newest equipment and technologies and equally invest in training the people who operate the machines and control the processes."

As Jeannine Kunz, SME's vice president of Tooling U-SME, and vice president, director of training and development, told me, "Manufacturing may be riding the digital wave, but waves will quickly go away when your operations side of the house can't deliver orders.

We especially need to train and support operators who can get products out the door." Over time, Kunz says that she and her team "realized that creating content was the easy part. We needed to go a step farther as the market needed content to be translated into a plan for their workforce. We actually added a team that provides learning consultants to our member companies." For example, in addressing AM, SME works with the manufacturers to determine how it fits into the production process, how to create quality programs specifically for AM, and write job descriptions for AM operators and technicians. Technical classes and certifications are but one component of the total training solution. She added, "The conversation now is more robust and collaborative to the point that we have added the TuXperience, an event where our community shares how people solve workforce problems in order to advance the industry."

How to Attract Talent to Manufacturing

For many years, the SME Foundation has been reaching out to high schools to attract talent for manufacturing, funding 140 students with $400,000 in scholarships. However, with the increasing skills gap, it was clear that while scholarships were a good step, they were not driving change at the heart of the problem. In 2011, the Partnership Response In Manufacturing Education initiative was formed. Since then PRIME has grown from six high schools to 44 in 22 states. Kunz explained: "SME directed some of the scholarships to the trades and more importantly, realized that in class there has to be integration of equipment with curriculum." SME does the heavy lifting on creating plans, curriculum and programs, while industry provides the financial support. Companies that want to support the program donate funds that are designated to specific schools tied to the company's manufacturing interests, such as geographic locations where their manufacturing operations are based.

The community and the company then conduct a needs assessment with SME staff to evaluate what additions are needed for a successful program. Support ranges from starting a program from scratch to bolstering an existing facility. "What is unique," said Kunz, "is that the kinds of things we bring in are generic enough to benefit the entire ecosystem in the community, so that graduates can move easily between manufacturing workforce opportunities." Some of the schools have a model factory floor or a job shop that covers every aspect of production, including sales and quality control.

CHAPTER FIFTEEN
An Apprenticeship for the Digital Age

Suchit Jain, Dassault Systemes Solidworks vice president for strategy and business development, suggested that I look into Tethys Engineering as an example of an innovative workforce training program, and he was spot-on in his recommendation. Founded by engineer Frederic Ramioulle, who was exposed to the European apprenticeship model as a student in Belgium, Tethys' is an engineering apprenticeship for the digital age. Jain calls it Uber for Engineering, but with student profiles and the ability to communicate, it also projects a LinkedIn style. "Like in Germany, we had five to six hours of practical hands-on application workshops on top of morning classes," he explained. "And the apprenticeships are closely aligned with local industry for the best student introduction to the real world." Ramioulle realized that at local colleges there was not enough sustained business to support student interns, so instead, they get summer jobs at Walmart, which doesn't advance their learning. Since so much engineering in the digital age happens online, especially in the design phase, he thought there would be an opportunity for both students and businesses to work together via an online platform. The first software partnership happens to be with Solidworks, which is a design tool that has penetrated many college campuses. Engineering students were already familiar with Solidworks and its application in manufacturing.

"Interestingly," Ramioulle observed, "employers think students can't contribute. But really, how do they think students will be less clueless when suddenly they get a diploma? Knowledge does not go from zero to 100 percent upon graduation." At first it was difficult to get businesses to register, but after a few months the online program ramped up. The customers who came on board first were small companies because they found that the engineers were affordable. Being located in the Phoenix area, Ramioulle had recruited quite a few Arizona State students who were in top-notch degree programs. To sustain business, he wanted to keep pricing low to compete with India. Most important, he wanted a large percentage of the fees to go directly to the students.

The first companies were surprised by how much the students could accomplish. But with defined task parameters and good communication, that is exactly what one would expect from a new engineering hire. The start-up platform is beginning to get some serious traction with the sign-up of ZF TRW, the $32 billion automotive components supplier, rewarding Ramioulle's hard work and belief in young people. "Tethys is one of most satisfying things I've done," he said. "The benefit people feel has been tremendous. If we want to care for the next generation, we need to change and push systems. There is no limit to what our children can do if we give them a chance and give them the right coaching." When Tethys gets to critical volume, Ramioulle hopes to expand the crowd sourcing aspect of the platform, with more interaction between mentors/coaches, students and businesses, so that everyone can learn in the process.

PART FOUR

Recommendations for Manufacturers

Fostering interest in STEM and STEAM education and entrepreneurship in schools must be a primary focus for us all if innovation that improves the world is to continue. Increasingly, we're seeing programming ideas that are turning education on its head in an attempt to address what it means to live in a connected, digital world. More and more companies are stepping up to the plate, partnering with educational visionaries to ensure they have in place the workers they will need to drive technology forward in the development of new products.

When MIT's CBA and a group of advocates formed the Fab Foundation in 2009 to focus on development of new fab labs and support for existing labs, they were lucky. Sherry Lassiter, who worked for CBA, happened to have achieved a master's degree from Harvard's esteemed School of Education, and she intuitively understood the connection between digital fabrication and instruction. She has been the perfect choice as the Fab Foundation's leader, integrating formal K-12 educational programming with the fab lab community. Her work has attracted leading corporations, including Chevron and GE, help-ing the Fab Lab Network drive innovation in education programs.

CHAPTER SIXTEEN
Chevron Invests in Future Workers

As part of a larger investment in nonprofits that are changing the training landscape, Chevron pledged $10 million to the Fab Foundation in order to install both stationary and mobile fab labs in communities that needed a STEM education boost. From the Carnegie Science Center in Pittsburgh, to Odessa College in Odessa, Texas, and from Fab Lab DC in our nation's capitol to California State University in Bakersfield, Calif., Chevron funding has given organizations the tools they need to change their communities and deliver the promise of next-generation education.

The Chevron Corp. has been more than just a generous fab lab

Blair Blackwell, Chevron's manager of education and corporate programs (left), and Sherry Lassiter, President of the Fab Foundation at SXSW 2017 in Austin, Texas. Courtesy of P. Boisvert.

financial sponsor. In collaboration with the Fab Foundation, Chevron has become an active advocate of the power of fab labs in fostering STEM education in local communities, as well as on national media platforms. Through Chevron's efforts, former "MythBusters" television show co-host Adam Savage is touring maker cities in the United States in order to document innovation in education, entrepreneurship and workforce development. Growing out of the White House "Maker Initiative" during the Obama administration, the tour has Savage stopping in at local fab labs, maker spaces and schools with a video team. Although the visits generate a lot of buzz when they occur, the ability to share the experience via multiple media channels expands the impact nationwide, showcasing making and its connection to creative inventions. As an engineering company, Chevron's focus is centered on innovation, so the collaborative nature of the relationship with the Fab Foundation is a natural fit. Blair Blackwell, Chevron's manager of education and corporate programs, explained that "Chevron was particularly attracted to being a part of the Fab Lab Network because fab labs allow opportunities for community members to come up with an idea and see that idea come to life. We specifically want to make sure students have that opportunity and then help them see how those kinds of skills are going to help them in their future careers. With hands-on, engaging student participation, fab labs bring science and engineering to life for kids."

Blackwell says that the interactive, collaborative nature of the Fab Lab Network easily lends itself to coordinating new labs in diverse locations. "We wanted the new fab labs to have a common set of tools that also provide the flexibility for a local community to adapt the technologies for their own needs. Plus, the Fab Lab Network is a vibrant community, and we wanted to be a part of that energy!" The Chevron team spent about a year evaluating the best strategy for investing in STEM education, including visiting the Fab Lab at the MC2 STEM High School in Cleveland. Blackwell was impressed because "to see a fab lab in action brings home just how engaging and exciting the hands-on learning opportunities can be for students. Talking to kids who had experienced the process helped us see that there were not enough connections between what the students were learning in the classroom and real-world applications. That's where we want to have impact."

The first Chevron-funded fab lab was launched at California State University, Bakersfield. The new fab lab served as a platform for another Chevron STEM program, Project Lead the Way. Blackwell said "It was especially exciting as we were able to pair middle-school students from Project Lead the Way with the fab lab at the University. The students work in the classroom with engineering design processes and then get to see their work come to life at the fab lab. Hearing, 'When can we come back?' from the students told us we were spot-on in the opportunities for students." The fab lab is now the favorite place for these kids to test, design and learn. In the future, high-school students will also be included.

The investment is paying off. At the end of 2016, the six completed Fab Lab Centers reported that over 20,000 people benefited from STEM education activities with an impressive 44.1 percent female participation. The Chevron investment also pulled in $1.4 in supplemental direct funding from local community sources, leveraging the initial dollars to further expand programming. These numbers, of course, do not account for the additional people reached through public events and media outlets, raising awareness of STEM and STEAM education programs and their importance for the vibrancy of cities, states and neighborhoods.

Blackwell reiterated that for Chevron, the fab lab funding is not only a philanthropic endeavor but also, perhaps more important, an investment in future workers. "In this day and age, corporate education investment is imperative. Companies work best when we have increasing diversity in the STEM pipeline. We feel we cannot neglect K-12 training when looking for a diverse and well-qualified workforce. For us, this is a long-term investment looking far out into the future, so we need to reach back to lower grades to be sure we are preparing students today to be the innovators of tomorrow."

In looking toward the Brilliant Factory concept described earlier, GE also recognized the need for a skilled workforce. Employing 290,000 people, many of whom function in technical roles, the manufacturer a few years ago established an online matchmaking platform called the GE Brilliant Career Lab. There students can enter information that uses algorithms to match them with potential careers, and then they can learn exactly what that job entails on a detailed, daily basis. Courses in the platform offer digital badges in critical thinking, teamwork and other topics that look good on an entry-level resume.

Wanting to bring the online experience to Boston where GE has re-located its headquarters and will need high-quality staff, the company partnered with the Boston Public Schools and the Fab Foundation. The Fab Foundation had outfitted several mobile fab labs for various parts of the nation and recently, as part of the Chevron mission, it realized that a mobile fab lab could be a real-world extension of the GE Brilliant Career Lab website. Once students have found an interesting career possibility, they could go into the fab lab and try out corresponding tools, such as 3D printers, design software and laser cutters. The new GE Brilliant Career Lab on wheels can now be seen in the Boston area visiting schools, colleges and innovation centers, sparking interest in STEM careers that exactly fit a student's interests.

CHAPTER SEVENTEEN
Communities and Educators Get Involved

As often happens, synergy between Chevron and GE corporate goals led to a collaboration with the Fab Foundation on a bigger, international STEM project. "We realized early on that schools were pulling for using fab labs in STEM education, but everyone was starting in a silo," observed Sherry Lassiter. "And the schools without curriculum, lesson plans and professional development were often not using the machines." Both Chevron and GE wanted to bring together a strong community of practice composed of formal educators who are interested in leveraging new digital fabrication technologies to teach STEM, and so the SCOPES-DF platform was born. Lassiter explained, "We combine pioneering educators with master fabricators to bring the entire community together to figure out what works. Then we share freely online so that there is a powerful way for the community to connect and leverage each other's work."

In the first phase, the SCOPES-DF team is pulling together great pioneering ideas through a formal vetting process and then linking to national standards. The concepts are tested in classroom settings.

For the second phase, the educational tools will be embedded in at least three school districts. SCOPES-DF will then work with teachers and administrators to design bottom-up strategies and frameworks to integrate into the work they're doing already. Perhaps most important, the results in this phase will be used to build with educators the professional development needed to scale. Disseminating programs and scaling will take up the third phase with feedback loops of continuous improvement. Interestingly, SCOPES-DF will add an anthropologist in each school to document the process so that scaling is possible.

I met Real World Scholars at the 2017 South by Southwest Education Conference in Austin, Texas. It was serendipity that I sat next to its co-founder John Cahalin at a Fab Foundation/Chevron presentation. He invited me to a panel that RWS was hosting, and it turned out that one of the panelists was Dr. Todd Keruskin, assistant superintendent of the Elizabeth Forward School District in the Greater Pittsburgh area. We know Dr. Keruskin because the school district is home to, you guessed it, a fab lab. The panel was fascinating not because of the cool tools Dr. Keruskin's class used, but because elementary and middle-school kids were practicing actual entrepreneurship.

Cahalin explained to me that the RWS Foundation gave each teacher $1,000 to start a small business in the classroom and helped them with the sales platform and marketing, taking no percentage of the revenues. The kids had to go through every aspect of a business from designing the product to production and then marketing and selling it. The group decided where to put its profits, which gave the project impact for the community. Dr. Keruskin's students donated their profits to a student who had a rare genetic disease, helping ease the financial burden on her family. Dr. Keruskin reminisced that in shop class, everyone made the same birdhouse, and not one of his classmates cared about birds. How different education can be when learning about things central to our everyday lives.

Dan Ryder from Farmington, Maine, started his freshman humanities class on an RSW entrepreneurship path, although that might not seem as logical as for a math or science class. But Ryder, who could have an alternate career as a comedian should he ever leave teaching, saw logic in applying to the program. He defended his choice: "Entrepreneurship marries well with English class. After all, design-thinking is an approach and a mindset. We solve most problems through communication skills, so it's a natural fit." Using design-thinking methodology, the class decided to design and 3D-print stress relief fidget gadgets. For Ryder, the experience was less about the financial outcome but more about learning and how that will move his students forward in life.

The entire room broke into tears when first-grade teacher Ashley Greenway from rural Rome, Ga., described her little children's "business." First-graders have limited capabilities, so making soaps and scrubs was easy enough to be achievable but with enough market demand to generate revenue. Greenway made things manageable for the children — for example, pricing and packaging with number sequences that they had already learned in class, like multiples of ten. Since shipping was nationwide, geography became part of the learning experience, as the orders were graphed and mapped. Problem-solving was a huge part of the learning experience, as unexpected challenges had to be faced. The proud young founders of Sugar Kids Beauty eventually had $30,000 in profit to distribute, which is pretty amazing for a Title 9 school where 15 percent of the student population is homeless. Ashley said, "The transformative piece for kids is identifying needs in the community. They chose to fund a food kitchen and had enough money to supply food for six months. Making things and selling them through the RSW instilled in very young people that they could be change agents in their world."

CHAPTER EIGHTEEN
Putting Play Back Into Learning and Innovation

What exactly is the fascination with Lego bricks? When I was consulting for CBA at MIT and the Fab Foundation in Cambridge, I had an office at the Cambridge Innovation Center. The fourth-floor kitchen and lounge was always the busiest, I suspect because it had a Lego wall that begged everyone to be a kid again. Some of the designs were actually pretty amazing. Lego, the 50-year-old family-owned Danish company, is the largest toy company in the world, and today the brightly colored plastic pieces are also being used to make prosthetic devices, architectural models and, of course, to teach STEM subjects to children. I think the simplicity of the design is what touches our aesthetic sense, plus, they are ridiculously easy to use. No classes or instructions are needed. Any child intuitively knows what to do when they have more than one Lego piece. The simplicity also means that Lego bricks can make whatever you imagine, since the building blocks are the most fundamental level of making something. And you can't deny that bright colors are more fun than ironsides gray.

My most favorite trade show swag ever is a USB drive from SME at the RAPID Conference that is attached to brightly colored Lego pieces. My mission at RAPID was then to find an extra one so I could join them together and play during downtime. Such fun! Lego is committed to how play affects us as humans and has been a financial supporter of the MIT Media Lab since about the time it opened in 1985. Lego is interested in expanding what they call "playful learning" through hands-on activities that develop problem-solving, critical thinking and creativity. These are exactly the research areas being explored at MIT by Dr. Seymour Papert, the mathematician who predicted in the last century that we'd be teaching math and other subjects to kids through their own personal computers. The Lego-endowed professorship at the Media Lab was first held by Dr. Papert and is now named in his honor and held by Professor Mitchel Resnick. Dr. Papert saw an interrelationship between learning, play and technology in his work on constructionism theory, which is closely related to problem-based learning, although perhaps with more nuance.

Research at MIT's Media Lab is always at the frontier of new thought in a field, and Lego's funding of research, faculty chairs and graduate student fellows in the Media Lab has been instrumental in advancing the study of play. One of the projects to emerge from the collaboration derived from MIT's programmable brick technology. Embedding tiny electronics into an ordinary Lego brick adds functionality that makes building and programming things such as robots much easier. In 1998, the next generation of Lego bricks was commercially launched in the

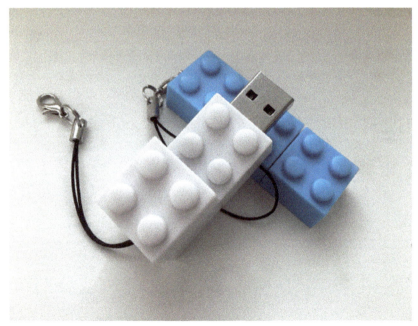

Lego Thumb Drives Compliments SME. Courtesy of P. Boisvert.

MindStorms product, affectionately named after Dr. Papert's landmark book.

MIT is committed to community outreach and in this digital age has made many opportunities available to educators and to the general public. Videos, webinars, hackathons and online courses from projects and departments supplement the free MITx digital course offerings. In the area of "playful learning," Michael Resnick, the Lego Papert Professor of Learning Research at MIT, leads a research group with the delightful name, Lifelong Kindergarten. The group developed Scratch, a coding platform for kids. Community engagement includes Scratch Day, Computer Clubhouse, a Scratch online community and my personal favorite, the Duct Tape Network. Most recently, professor Resnick and his students have launched a free online course, "Learning Creative Learning," that gives people of all ages concepts, tools and pathways to developing creative learning in themselves and their organizations. Hands-on activities are a key part of the course, as is developing community connections. At FabLabHub, we plan to organize local meetups in the lab to learn together from the videos and then implement what we learned with our fab lab tools. I am particularly interested in bringing entrepreneurs into our group to disrupt how they think about learning in their start-ups. Flexibility of the program is very appealing for our over-programmed lives, and the course can be completed at your own pace. Special video conferencing tools called "Unhangouts" will provide the ability to interact with other participants.

CHAPTER NINETEEN
A Word About the Future of Manufacturing

There exists an intermediary step between how we manufacture things today and the "Star Trek" replicator, when anything will be available at our fingertips right in our homes. 3D printing is decades away from one machine generating products made from every type of material, and even if we could make anything at home, I am not sure everyone wants to do so. I have many friends with enviable gourmet kitchens who don't cook. I could buy a digital sewing machine to make readily available Armani patterns, but I'd look like a bag lady, as I have no talent, patience or interest in that department. Terry Wohlers, a marketing consultant in the 3D printing area, and I agree: Computers replaced analog activities that we were already doing, like keeping a paper address book or calendar. But most people today are not usually making their own things at home. A shift in attitude needs to happen first, which we are just starting to see in the digital natives who are being exposed to making in school and at makerspaces.

"Distributed manufacturing" purports to be the next step in this path away from global manufacturing. There are some variations in its definition that I confirmed with my friend Anna Waldman-Brown, whose graduate work in technology policy at MIT revolves around digital fabrication and manufacturing production. The purest distributed manufacturing seems to be when goods are produced and consumed locally as opposed to being shipped around the world. But there are broader definitions, including Waldman-Brown's research focus on small-batch production on a large scale.

We're seeing extraordinary examples of local economies taking hold of their livelihoods, which does require that customers are willing to modify shopping behavior to participate in the new system. For example, I am a strong advocate of my local farmer's market, mostly because, having grown up in a food-centric, old-world family, I think the food tastes better. Plus, it's a great place to make new, like-minded friends. I also shop there because I sense something is wrong with eating blueberries year-round that were grown very far away. But it means I have to plan better, since the market is only open on Saturday and Tuesday mornings, with a small contingent selling on Wednesday afternoons. Fresh, organic produce goes bad quickly, so timing my shopping trips takes serious consideration and, one hopes that the market hours

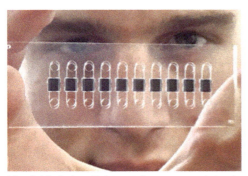

Microfluidic device with integrated sensors, manufactured by Potomac Photonics. Courtesy of Potomac Photonics, Inc.

fit with one's work schedule. Since production levels are low, I have to get there early, usually at 7:30 a.m. in order to get best choice from my favorite tomato, cucumber, cheese, peach and green chili vendors before they sell out. Since most areas of the United States can't grow blueberries in winter, I also modify my cooking patterns and try to stay with what's in season. Oh, and by the way, I am also willing to pay more in dollars in addition to the time it takes to support the ecosystem, although I do wish there was more convenience built into the process, which would add more value to the pricing.

Standards for Distributed Manufacturing

Having built medical devices during my tenure at Potomac Photonics, I understand too well the rigors of manufacturing FDA-approved products. I cannot imagine some maker producing cardiac stents in his garage, and I certainly wouldn't want them in my body. Although I feel that America has become too litigious, some degree of quality control in the medical device, pharmaceuticals and biotech industries makes me feel safer. Certain products may never be good candidates for totally distributed manufacturing, since quality control is, in fact, essential to the very essence of the product. I've heard a story of someone placing an order for some things from five different, good-sized maker spaces. Not one was able to deliver the required quantity at the agreed date with acceptable product specifications. Perhaps maker spaces in general are still not the place to go for professional quality manufacturing, although there are excellent examples earlier in this book of rapid prototyping success. I can say from experience that the leap to volume production requires more than just adding workers; it requires a change in operations mindset and execution.

That said, a few examples of distributed manufacturing are making headway:

- **Aker**, a company mentioned earlier, digitally ships designs to makers who can create an urban garden, locally using local tools, although the company does offer analog shipping of manufactured products.

- **Fab Lab House**, developed by the Institute of Advanced Architecture of Catalonia, is a digitally designed and fabricated solar house that won the Public's Choice Award at the European Solar Decathlon 2010. The parameters of the structure are digitally modified to adhere to the geographic conditions where the pre-fabricated parts are assembled. The design files can be purchased from Barcelona and CNC-machined in Colorado, where the parts can be assembled in a totally different environment but with similar energy savings. Also, the house is pretty cool-looking and it is functional for everyday living.

- The **Thingiverse** platform started by MakerBot to grow the consumer 3D-printing market offers both as free, open-source designs and paid designs, and it has recently added a marketplace for ready-made goods. But the maker market, while enthusiastic, is still small.

- **Enabling the Future** is a worldwide collective of volunteers who 3D print prosthetic hands at significantly lower cost than healthcare companies can manufacture devices, then give them away to those in need. While some of the recipients can get the hands to function properly, those without training from a therapist or a good support system end up putting the hand in a drawer. There is wide variation in quality. Having tried to reduce the hand size for some tiny children in India, an intern in my lab discovered that printing hands is not a trivial undertaking. Every 3D printer is calibrated differently and operated by a maker with varying expertise, which adds to problems in part repeatability and consistency. Members of the group are working to refine online designs and to widen the types of prosthetics that are available, which has helped considerably. Enabling the Future has shed light on the power of distributed manufacturing. Many examples can be found in the community where gross motor skills, such as throwing a ball or picking up a water cup, have enormous impact on recipients' lives. The success stories capture the imagination and, it is hoped, will increase financial support for the nonprofit. But the operational details are still in the development stage.

Veterans Have a Role

With its built-in infrastructure and professional-level expertise, a new public-private partnership between the Department of Veterans Affairs Center for Innovation (VACI) and 3D-printing manufacturer Stratasys may have a greater chance of distributed manufacturing success. To kick off the program, the equipment manufacturer will provide 3D printers, materials, support and training to five strategically chosen

VA hospitals: in Puget Sound, San Antonio, Albuquerque, Orlando and Boston. A couple of key points give this project legs. First, the hospitals will be fully integrated, allowing for easy transfer of design files and expertise for shared learning. Second, Stratasys is providing training. As in classrooms, giving medical personnel equipment based on new technologies without training and know-how is incomplete generosity.

Advances in body armor for today's soldier and better field triage means more veterans are returning home alive but with missing limbs. 3D printing of orthotics, prosthetics and fairings will assist the VA in serving a growing veteran population. While the heart-warming sto-ries of 3D-printed prostheses grab the media headlines, the VA proj-ect will also focus on anatomical models used today for improving surgical outcomes while reducing costs. Surgeons, physicians, nurs-es and other medical staff can also be trained more easily with the help of 3D models. The National Institutes of Health also offers on-line resources. The NIH 3D Print Exchange is another example of

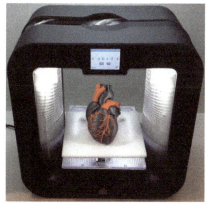

While Fab Lab Hub only 3D printed a model heart, bio-printing is not too far into the future. Courtesy of P. Boisvert.

medical distributed manufacturing. A few years ago, a group of sci-entists at the government agency and other nonprofits realized there was a growing need for easily accessible medical and biological mod-els. Design is often the biggest barrier to using 3D printing, especially for things as complex as the human heart or some bacterium. The 3D Print Exchange is open source and interactive with designs provided through a crowd-sourcing platform. It gives researchers, students and educators optimized files that can be downloaded and printed, enhanc-ing medical treatment and education on the local level.

Many argue that the Henry Ford model of a production line creating everything in one factory can be replaced with many smaller craft centers that reduce shipping costs and improve quality of life for employees or owner/operators while they build local economies. It is hard to find good examples of this model where pricing can compete with high-volume production. People point to Etsy, the online store for crafts, but most of the shops are small, and prices are typically at the art-and-craft level. I was recently at a meeting where Etsy management was looking to match its shop owners with manufacturers who could deliver higher volume than a designer could by making products in their kitchen or garage. Etsy may be a potential model for local maker-space production facilities, but again, the market size is still comparatively small, limiting economic competitiveness. I personally prefer the uniqueness of handcrafted items, but most of the world does not have the financial ability to pay more for the same function as a mass-produced item.

IKEA has hit on a great marketing concept by making cool, Euro-chic products at ridiculously low prices, marrying uniqueness with affordability. At Fab12 in Shenzhen, we witnessed the well-oiled machine that is Chinese mass manufacturing of anything that one could ever want in electronics and consumer goods. In the service sector, however, we are seeing somewhat more success with distributed principles. For example, 3D Hubs matches customers with a local 3D printing expert — in my opinion, faster and easier than 3D printing yourself — based on job requirements. 3D Print Life Support matches 3D printer owners who need service or technical support with local technicians. Both are thriving programs that bring a service solution right to your neighborhood. From an ecological standpoint it makes far more sense to manufacture locally, but the desire to make has not yet developed to a point where this is viable for mainstream markets, and economic models have not yet caught up.

At least in the foreseeable future, smart manufacturing is the answer for mass production. And that takes workers skilled for new collar jobs.

CHAPTER TWENTY
Seize the Opportunity

To those who say the skills gap is a problem, I say, innovate and excel! We live in a time of extraordinary opportunity to look to the future and fundamentally change manufacturing jobs but also to show people the value in new collar jobs and to create non-traditional pathways to engaging, fulfilling careers in the digital factory. If industry is to invigorate and revitalize manufacturing, it must start with the new collar workers who essentially make digital fabrication for Industry 4.0 possible.

Concepts such as 3D printing, robots, self-driving cars and the colonization of Mars are changing what once was science fiction to fact in our daily lives. Manufacturing is no different. Big data, automation, additive manufacturing, generative design and virtual reality have digitized the factory floor, which now demands a new collar skillset of its workforce. Manufacturers want an agile, engaged staff that is first and foremost able to solve problems in this rapidly changing environment. More specifically, today's operator or technician must also be able to handle arithmetic, geometry and basic algebra, read, interpret and modify a CAD file, understand machine tool path, use measurement tools for quality control programs and gather/analyze big data coming from the IoT. These are the types of skills that moved blue collar jobs to the digital new collar job era.

To fill new collar jobs, we desperately need new education models. Kids today are more independent and less likely to follow a traditional system. Model programs such as those in fab labs, SME PRIME classrooms, and maker spaces intrinsically build the skills that manufacturers say they need with hands-on, problem-based learning methodologies. Success stories abound, and now the methods from those examples need to be shared to help other groups bring new collar job training to their communities.

Perhaps the hardest skill for most people is adapting easily to change. Resistance to change is often driven by fear of the unknown and how it will affect us and our immediate circle of friends, family and colleagues. In my experience, true innovation is an ability to reach beyond fear of failure or ridicule to try something totally new and different. It is only innovation in our processes, methodologies, institutions and tools that will advance meaningful solutions to employment problems. It is my firm belief that innovation drives problem-solving for all issues. Doing things the same old way doesn't usually amount to much progress and merely sweeps the fundamental root cause of a problem to a dark corner where it invariably festers.

But do not fear. A few creative groups who are embracing change are experimenting with new models that are not too radically unlike previous successes. Apprenticeships in Germany have been around since the Middle Ages, and several new collar job training programs are not too different from them. Problem sets have been used at MIT and other universities for years to train highly sought-after graduates who have made a huge impact on our world. Innovation can build on past successes. While it may have a new name or look somewhat different, the principles of new collar job training often have already been proven.

In overcoming fear, it is useful to communicate with and face whatever it is that scares us and open a discourse. I'd strongly suggest that if you want to effect change in education and workforce training, you visit any one of the impactful programs discussed in this book. They are in every part of the country, so it shouldn't be too hard to find a site nearby. It's also easy to participate online with some of the university programs, as well as with Fab Lab Hub's online DigiFab Alliance. Or better yet, to meet many change makers in one place, attend a Maker Faire or DigiFabCon.

When we open our minds to new possibilities, we find change is not so scary after all. In this case, the very survival of manufacturing, our companies and our people depends on building the foundation of new collar jobs, and we must do it now.

References

[1] https://obamawhitehouse.archives.gov/sites/default/files/ microsites/ostp/fact_sheet_final.pdf

[2] https://www.bls.gov/opub/mlr/2015/article/stem-crisis-or-stem-surplus-yes-and-yes.htm

[3] https://www2.deloitte.com/us/en/pages/manufacturing/articles/ global-manufacturing-competitiveness-index.html

[4] http://www.themanufacturinginstitute.org/~/media/ 827DBC76533942679A15EF7067A704CD.ashx

[5] Tom Morrison, Bob Maciejewski, Craig Giffi, Emily Stover DeRocco, Jennifer McNelly, and Gardner Carrick, Boiling point? The skills gap in U.S. manufacturing (Washington, DC, and New York: The Manufacturing Institute and Deloitte, 2011)

[6] Infographic at http://www.manpowergroup.com/ talent-shortage-2016

[7] http://www.nytimes.com/2012/11/18/opinion/sunday/ Friedman-You-Got-the-Skills.html?ref=todayspaper&_r=0

[8] https://hbr.org/2012/12/who-can-fix-the-middle-skills-gap

[9] https://gbc.org/wp-content/uploads/2016/01/ GBC-ABC-STEM-report-2016.pdf

[10] America's Most Wanted: Skilled Workers; http://www.nutsand-boltsfoundation.org

[11] https://www2.deloitte.com/content/dam/Deloitte/us/Documents/ manufacturing/us-public-perception-manufacturing-study.pdf

[12] http://www.sme.org/manufacturing-myths-infographic/

[13] Internal presentation to Massachusetts Manufacturing Community of Practice

[14] http://www.businessinsider.com/ibm-automated-future-new-collar-jobs-2017-1

[15] https://www.bizjournals.com/boston/news/2016/10/07/viewpoint-from-assembly-line-to-digital-thread-the.html

[16] http://www.marketsandmarkets.com/Market-Reports/smart-factory-market-1227.html

[17] https://www.siemens.com/innovation/en/home/pictures-of-the-future/industry-and-automation/digital-factories-defects-a-vanishing-species.html

[18] https://www.wired.com/story/google-glass-2-is-here/

[19] https://hbr.org/2017/03/augmented-reality-is-already-improving-worker-performance

[20] https://www.forrester.com/report/How+Enterprise+Smart+Glasses+Will+Drive+Workforce+Enablement/-/E-RES133722

[21] https://www.sas.com/content/dam/SAS/en_us/doc/research2/iw-iot-finding-path-to-value-108081.pdf

[22] http://us.talentlens.com/wp-content/uploads/TalentLens-Manufacturing-Shift-In-Skills.pdf

[23] http://blog.indeed.com/2017/01/17/cybersecurity-skills-gap-report/

[24] https://www.nytimes.com/2016/12/14/business/smallbusiness/veterans-san-diego-start-ups-entrepreneurs.html?_r=0

Resources

Fab Lab Hub

For help in starting or supporting a Fab Lab in the United States; to reach Sarah Boisvert; to find New Collar Job Training in the United States; for online training; to participate in the North American Digital Fabrication Alliance.
www.fablabhub.org
service@fablabhub.org
@NewCollarJobs

America Makes
The flagship Institute for Manufacturing USA, the National Network for Manufacturing Innovation can provide anything one needs to know about additive manufacturing and 3D printing.
https://www.americamakes.us

Center for Bits and Atoms at MIT
For information on Director Neil Gershenfeld and team's projects, publications and events.
www.CBA.MIT.EDU

DigiFab Conference
Program information for the annual digital fabrication Conference exploring how new technologies are changing the world; sponsorship or expo exhibit opportunities.
www.DigiFabCon.org
@DigiFabCon

Fab Foundation
For help in starting or supporting a Fab Lab anywhere in the world and the SCOPES-DF STEM education project.
www.fabfoundation.org

International Fab Lab List
To find an official Fab Lab in the Fab Lab Network associated with the Center for Bits and Atoms at MIT.
www.Fablabs.io

Laser Institute of America
For laser safety, laser materials processing and other technical training.
www.lia.org

Potomac Photonics, Inc.
www.Potomac-Laser.com

SME
For manufacturing training and high school PRIME program.
www.sme.org

About the Author

Sarah Boisvert has more 30 years of experience in the design, development and commercialization of high technology products utilizing digital fabrication, including laser machining and 3D printing. Her graduate work in market segmentation at Johns Hopkins University led to her expertise in productization of high-tech devices. Ms. Boisvert is a co-founder of the commercial division of Potomac Photonics, Inc. of Lanham, Md., which she joined to commercialize a proprietary RF-discharge excimer laser. Following the sale of the company in 1999, Ms. Boisvert founded Fab Lab Hub, part of the MIT-based Fab Lab Network, in order to foster entrepreneurship and workforce training in digital fabrication manufacturing skills. Since 2010, Fab Lab Hub has produced DigiFabCon, a conference and Fab Festival dedicated to demonstrating how digital fabrication is changing the world. During this time she also consulted for the Fab Foundation, the nonprofit organization that supports more than 1,200 Fab Labs worldwide. There she developed strategic plans, implemented marketing communication and conducted fundraising. She returned to Potomac part-time as Chief 3D Printing Officer in February 2014. In 2016, Ms. Boisvert conducted a study — partially funded by a contribution from the Verizon Foundation — into digital skills needed for operators and technicians in manufacturing. For the study, she interviewed leaders at 200 companies ranging in size from start-ups to Fortune 100 multi-nationals from a wide variety of industries. The data resulting from her work is the basis of this book. Ms. Boisvert is a Fellow and Past President of the Laser Institute of America and has served on the Optical Society of America's Industry Advisory Board, as well as on the boards of numerous international technical societies. For fun, she creates 3D-printed jewelry.

Index

CPSIA information can be obtained
at www.ICGtesting.com
Printed in the USA
LVHW07s1719130618
580602LV00028B/259/P